A Childhood Like Ou

A Childhood Like Ours...

Memories of Bungay in the 1950s

by

Terry Reeve

A Childhood Like Ours...

A Childhood Like Ours...
Copyright © Terry Reeve 2009

All rights reserved.

No part of this book may be reproduced in any form by photocopying or any electronic or mechanical means, including information storage or retrieval systems, without permission in writing from both the copyright owner and the publisher of the book.

ISBN 978-184426-605-0

Cover design by Penny Reeve

First Published 2009 by
FASTPRINT SILVER PUBLISHING
Peterborough, England.

Printed on FSC approved paper by
www.printondemand-worldwide.com

A Childhood Like Ours…

Cover picture: The author and two of his brothers, Chris and Robin, presenting a play on the make-shift stage in front of the garden shed in the early 1950s; and Bungay children swimming in the River Waveney at the Falcon Meadow, in front of the Sea Scouts' boathouse.

Most pictures generously provided from the Bungay Town Recorder's collection.

A Childhood Like Ours...

A Childhood Like Ours…

Contents

Introduction	6
Fruit Picking	8
Shops	12
And More Shops	28
The Mayfair Cinema	34
Bungay Grammar School	38
St Mary's School	44
Stow Fen and Outney Common	51
The Side Gate	60
The Black Dogs	70
Shopping and Deliveries	76
The Shed	82
Indoors	88
The Trinity Rooms	92
Music and Dancing	97
Biking and Walking	100
Customs and Traditions	107
And then there Was…	112

A Childhood Like Ours…

Introduction

*S*OMEONE said to me the other day: "A childhood like ours doesn't happen any more…"
It struck me that if that is the case, it is very sad. But in these modern times where technological and electronic advances seem to gather ever more pace, probably it is true. And if it is, it is all the more important to record what our childhood was like, and what things and activities were significant to us.

I left Bungay in 1962 to start my working life as a newspaper reporter, the then Norfolk News Company dispatching me to its Cromer office. It was three weeks before I returned home for my first weekend off, and I remember that day as clearly as if it were yesterday. As I came across the Falcon Bridge from Ditchingham Dam and up Bridge Street towards the Market Place in the bus, a huge sense of contentment and well being came over me. I was back in Bungay, and all was well. I knew then that one day I would return there to live, though I didn't know it would be 23 years before I achieved it.

That innate love for Bungay had been nurtured through the first 19 years of my life since I was born in 1943 - so most of the formative years of my life were the 1950s.

It is the memories of those years that I have drawn on to write this book of Bungay in those days through a boy's eyes - not necessarily a typical boy, but one who was from a secure and happy home, who enjoyed life to the full and was brought up to be aware of things around him, and to appreciate them.

What did we do, what was important to us, what sports did we play, how did we occupy ourselves at home and in the garden as

A Childhood Like Ours…

youngsters, how did we earn our first pocket money, which facilities in the town did we make use of, what and where were our adventures, what was school like - what was Bungay like physically?

This book, a series of essays I suppose, looks at those things and more under a number of headings in an effort to evoke an atmosphere of ordinary, routine life for children in the town in the years when the country was recovering, as each year went by, from the privations and stress of the second world war. Some may seem trivial unless set against that background, but as children our parents encouraged us to write.

A typical memory for me, not included in the body of this book, is probably from around 1950. At school and at home the pencils we used were plain wooden pencils, often not even carrying the name of the maker on them. Then one Dad came home and gave me a pencil painted dark green. Such a simple thing, but I remember being in awe and excited about it. A tiny thing like that was somehow a symbol of how things were moving forward. And I wrote eagerly with it.

My mother, Iris Reeve, wrote a book of her memories of Bungay in the 1920s. Malcolm Bedingfield scribed his thoughts on the 1930s. Perhaps someone will write of the 1940s one day, or the 1960s.

In the meantime, here are some of my warm and happy memories, in no particular order, of the 1950s…

A Childhood Like Ours…

Fruit Picking

WHEN it comes to working in the school holidays today, what are the options? Stacking shelves in supermarkets, washing up or waitressing in pubs and restaurants, joining a cleaning team - and all the while being mindful of health and safety and public protection issues.

I was in a giant foodstore the other day where students were earning their holiday money and it struck me how lucky we were in the 1950s and able to go fruit picking, hourly paid or piecework - there were plenty of opportunities around Bungay and the Waveney Valley in those days, a short bike ride from home.

Red House Farm at Mettingham, run by the Berkeley-Smiths for example - that was my first experience of it, at the age of 11 or 12, going blackcurrant picking. I and my brother got on our bikes one morning and cycled to the field, which was at Shipmeadow, opposite St Bartholomew's Church and on the corner of the Low Road junction with the Beccles to Bungay road. There were other teenagers and many women in the gang there, picking the juicy black fruit in the field which sloped down the side of the valley towards the Waveney. There was a canvas shelter for the supervisors and the foreman, where the large scales were to weigh the baskets as you brought them in, and to tick off the number of baskets beside your name as a check on how many you had done. It was piece work, and I believe we got 9d for a basket weighing perhaps 4-5lbs.

We set to work. There were plenty of school friends to share banter with and talk about football, as the sun beat down from the blue summer sky and brought out strongly the aromas of the

8

A Childhood Like Ours…

fruit and the bushes and the soil beneath - a scent heightened by the purple juice stains which soon covered your hands.

The women picked much faster than us schoolboys - they were more nimble-fingered I suppose. It seemed to take ages to fill one of the cardboard, metal-handled baskets, and every so often the foreman, Sid - I don't know his other name but those who worked there will remember him - would come along the rows advising: "Pluck them bushes clean, t'gether - pluck'em clean."

Of course while the women did, we were not so conscientious - we got the best of the bunches and ignored the fiddly ones that did not fill the basket so quickly, and moved on to the next bush, or even turned round and started picking from the bushes in the next row beside us.

That annoyed Sid if he saw you as he made his rounds, and we would get stern warnings and be shown the fruit we had missed.

That first time I made 7s 6d - no matter that the women probably took home £1-£1.10s, it was a fortune to a young boy, and we pedalled home at the end of the day tired and satisfied. I probably bought the latest Famous Five book, from Spashett's in St Mary's Street, with the money.

On one occasion I was sent home for not "plucking them bushes clean," when Sid caught me picking from the row beside me. But we still went back again another day, to that idyllic setting in the fresh open air, and we got as brown as berries in the process. Sid still got frustrated with us from time to time, and when he took his trilby off to scratch his head he revealed a completely white, bald pate in stark contrast to his brown and weather-beaten face.

There was also strawberry and raspberry picking, and over at Orchard Farm at Barsham, bean-picking, and plum picking. We could earn good money there - even up to £1 a day sometimes - among the leaves of the plum trees. Sometimes we stuffed our

A Childhood Like Ours...

pockets full of fruit to take home - you couldn't do that with blackcurrants, raspberries or beans! But one day, leaving the orchard and having to cycle past the farmhouse, I saw there was a police car outside.

My young mind, with a dose of conscience, immediately surmised that they must be there because pickers had been stealing the fruit, and I stopped and hastily emptied my pockets of plums into the hedgerow, before cycling past.

No doubt, however, there was a much more mundane reason for the police car being there.

Later, from the mid-1950s, we got summer holiday work at Broome Fruit Farm, Mr Dupoix's place, picking apples. Many boys from the grammar school and secondary modern school were taken on there on a hourly paid basis during the holidays, to pick first Beauty of Bath, then Worcesters and later Laxtons. Coxes were not usually picked in earnest till after we had returned to school.

There was a regular group of women pickers, too - we all worked under the direction of Frank Honeywood, who was foreman there in those days, along with his brother Peter. And there was old Mr Rumsby, and Stan, a small Polish man who were regulars, too.

Our group of schoolboys included my brother Robin, Graham Patrick, David Redden, Robin Griffin, Alan Debenham, David and Peter Butcher, John Sturgeon, Stephen Rumsby, Peter Smith, and Jonathan and Sandy Wortley, among others.

They were halcyon days, sitting at the top of a ladder among the fruit, the branches shading you from the sun, munching apples to your hearts content. Because it was hourly paid, there was a lot of skiving (idling) done, but we always got the fruit in when needed. But the apples were so fresh and so tempting, and it was no exaggeration that most of us must have eaten 1lb to a pound

A Childhood Like Ours…

and a half a day of the choicest fruit in the orchard.

Those were the days of frequent lunch-time apple fights after we had sat in the dry grass on the edge of the fields beside the orchards and eaten our packed lunches and drunk out orange juice or orange squash; and of climbing the vertical ladder up the water tower which stood beside one of the orchards. We used to reckon it was 100ft high as we got to the top and sat there - in truth it was probably no more than 30-40ft. Even so, I don't know what health and safety would have said about that activity today, had anyone fallen. But we had no cares, and there was no sense of fear.

If it was wet and we had to abandon picking to wait for the rain to clear we would go into the rest room, and play cards - three-card brag usually, betting with our earnings. Some won and some lost, but I don't think anyone was out of pocket to any serious amount. And it passed the time until we were called out again.

I remember that my first week's wages for a 40-hour week - we started at 8am and finished at 5pm - amounted to £2 5s 2d. I was paid 1s 5d an hour as a 14-year-old, and I thought I was rich. The hours sometimes dragged, but on the whole it was fun - we were growing up, and I guess we learned something of life during the conversations and repartee and bonding song-singing that we did as we picked among the leaves and branches and tangy, fresh smell of fruit and the aromas of a rural Suffolk summer.

One of the songs we used to sing, with each one required, in turn, to add his own original verse following the chorus, was "Oh you'll never get to heaven…"

Looking back to those days, I sometimes think we were there, then...

Shops

SHOPS come and go in Bungay. There are those that remain only for a few months before closing, but there is always someone else prepared to have a go with a different commodity or service, and premises rarely stay empty for long, even in these difficult times for commerce.

It was not always so - as a schoolboy the shops seemed never to change, and I used to pass most of them on my way to school and back, from Southend Road to St Mary's School in Earsham Street.

Let me take you on that trip in, say, 1953...

Satchel on back, cap on head and sandals on feet, it took me from Southend Road into Laburnum Road, past Harry Read's builder's store in the old chapel. At the top of Laburnum Road at the junction with Bardolph Road there was a low, curved wall, on which I sat on the way home and waited for Dad to come home for dinner (that was midday meal in those days), and give me a ride on his bike crossbar the rest of the way. I used to pick chicory weeds while I waited, and break the stem to see the milky fluid come out. That little wall is still there today, though almost obscured by a hedge, but it reminds me still of sitting there waiting for Dad.

Crossing Bardolph Road into Upper Olland Street I passed the entrance to the Honeypot Meadow, where in the evening we used to kick a ball around. A five-barred gate was the entrance on the corner there, and people gathered to join the game. Around that time, while still attending St Mary's School, they began to build the police houses and police station on the site, and I was fascinated to watch the daily progress on the work, from foundations to completion, though it was the final end for a

A Childhood Like Ours…

popular playing field.

On along Upper Olland Street, past the Ministry of Food building (now the community centre), I crossed the road at the Vicarage (when Mum said goodbye she always added, "Have you got a handkerchief? Now cross the road at the Vicarage," and we dutifully did). Now it is Holmwood residential home for the elderly, but on the way home in the autumn we would gleefully crunch through the dry golden leaves from the chestnut trees in the Vicarage grounds, and dare to knock on the door to ask if we could get some conkers (they always let us). We stuffed our trouser pockets, blazer pockets, coat pockets and any other pockets we could find full of the polished, shiny brown fruit, and took it home to sort out the biggest ones for playing conkers in the playground the next day.

The wall of the Vicarage was made of flintstones, and once a year we would watch, as we passed, old Mr Nelson adding a new coat of tar to that wall. We could just about see the top, and marvelled at the broken pieces of glass sticking out of it, to deter trespassers. Today that wall is still as it was then, about 5ft high, tarred, and with the glass still there as security.

Over the road and then came the first shop - Myall's fish and chip shop, now a private house but until relatively recently an antiques shop and sewing business run by Colin Cook and his wife.

Next to that was the Rose and Crown pub, a traditional alehouse. Sometimes we would collect beer bottles - from where I can't remember - and take them there to claim the money back on them, 2d for each I think. Those were the days when beer bottles (and indeed Vimto and other soft drinks bottles) had metal caps on which were removed with a bottle opener. Inside the cap was a cork washer, and by removing that, putting the cap on your blazer lapel and pushing the cork back in from the other

13

side to secure it to the material, you could wear the top as a badge. I remember wearing a row of five or six such badges, all in different bright colours. Since it closed the Rose and Crown has had a number of uses, and for a time was a fish and ship shop, but is now a private house.

On down Upper Olland Street, the next shop was Percy Harmer's cycle repair shop. Percy was a lovely, kind and gentle chap, tall and slim, who always wore a cloth cap and blue boiler suit to work in his workshop at the back. He had a matching blue wool sock to cover the stump of one hand he lost in an accident, but it did not stop him repairing cycles. His shop had an earth floor, and he would let us go in there and scrabble in the earth to find ball bearings from cycle axles, which we used to make jumping beans. The idea was to carefully make a rough pouch with a piece of silver paper from a bar of chocolate or other confectionery, fold the edge over to seal it, put it in a matchbox and shake it for a while, and when you opened it, it would be a perfect jumping bean, shaped like a liquorice torpedo. When you rolled it out of the box is would jump along end to end. As children we found them absolutely fascinating. Percy, who loved having children around him, sold all sorts of things in that shop as well as cycle parts.

That shop is now a beauty salon, and is next door to Bardesley's Books. In the 1950s that premises was a private house, and beyond that was another fish and chip shop - another business that has been turned into a private house in recent years.

Ronnie Sampson's greengrocer's shop was on the corner of Rose Lane, which in the 1950s was Gas House Lane (in the 1960s the powers that be decided to change the name to a sweeter scent!). Ronnie was a popular character, well involved in the town's life, and it was a thriving business selling fruit, vegetables and flowers.

A Childhood Like Ours...

Past a house on the corner of Gas House Lane, you came to Edwards baker's shop, with its beautiful smell of new-baked bread, and cakes - mouth-watering cream doughnuts, cream horns, vanilla slices or coconut macaroons that we used to get as a treat, sometimes. Rene was the assistant who usually served in those days, always friendly, always smiling, as she wrapped the crusty loaves in tissue paper. In the list of favourite shops I passed on the way to school, that was up near the top.
Then there was Nursey's Sheepskin factory and shop - as it is now, the only shop at that stage of my walk still in the same use. Indeed the business has been more or less on the same site for over 200 years, since it was founded in 1790. The shop front has changed considerably and is now more modern, though traditionally so. The door and windows were blue, and above the shop, at right angles to it so it could easily be seen by everyone, was a large clock - very handy for those hurrying to work. I have reason to remember it with some embarrassment.
As a child, probably eight or nine I suppose, I got into a childish sulk after school one day and told Mum I was going to run away. We lived in Southend Road. I ran out of the gate, ran up Laburnum Road and over Bardolph Road in to Upper Olland Street, and up towards the town, not really knowing to where I was going. Eventually my run became a walk, to get my breath back, and as I walked I looked up, and saw that clock. It said five o'clock.
My walk turned to a loiter, and then I stopped, and thought, and felt hungry.
"Mmm," I thought to myself. "Five o'clock - nearly tea-time. I think I'll go home, and run away again after tea."
Of course after a hunger-sating tea the sulk, and running away, was forgotten.
A little way past Nursey's was a very small greengrocer's run

A Childhood Like Ours...

by Mr Rowe - a short wiry man with a very busy manner as he went in and out of the shop, putting produce into bags from the trays outside for his customers. That closed many years ago - it was roughly where Baird's the butcher's now is - until a few years ago it was Weaver and Dye's electrical goods shop.

Then came another bakery, Clarke's on the corner of Quave's Lane - one of five baker's shops in the town in those days. And on the opposite corner of Quave's Lane was the first shop in St Mary's Street, Twiddy's the grocer's, a small general store typical of the time, with things such as sugar sold loose, from a large tin from which the required amount was put into blue paper bags with a scoop, and weighed. Flour was sold in cloth sacks, biscuits were sold loose from tins and weighed out into brown paper bags, cheese was cut to the customer's requirements with a long wire - as children we were fascinated to watch it - and ham and bacon was sliced on a hand-operated slicer, so the customers could judge how many slices they wanted as they watched. Cling film and seal wrapping were not heard of in those days, and no one minded biscuits being served with ungloved hands.

Just past Twiddy's was Dowsing's furniture store, in the premises now occupied by a hair salon and the adjoining Country Pine. It was a large store, full of merchandise where Mr Dowsing, smartly dressed and with neat Brylcreemed hair, was always to be seen - he had two daughters, Delicia and Elizabeth I think, who went to St Mary's School.

From that premises to the corner of Priory Lane stretched another well-known business - Inward's bakery and restaurant. The baker's shop took up the space where the Indian restaurant now is, with the shop opening into the restaurant which occupied the space between bakery and Dowsing's (now taken up by Williams opticians, and 4-Nel Jewellers). It was well

A Childhood Like Ours...

St Mary's Street in the 1950s, with the former Inwards café on the left

patronised by local people and visitors, and the bakery was similar to the rest, with delicious crusty loaves filling the shelves and even more delicious - to us children - cream cakes, pies, biscuits, rusks, scones and all manner of confectionery.

The Bungay Co-op was on the opposite side of Priory Lane - it housed the ladies wear, menswear, children's wear and furniture department of the Co-operative Society, with the grocery and butchery side of the business being in Earsham Street (more of that later) though it was during the 1950s that the grocery department moved to Earsham Street and the furniture department closed, to be followed later by the clothing departments.

The Co-op was one of several shops in those days which seemed rather dark, with sombre lighting - certainly the men's and children's wear section, to the back and right of the building when facing it from St Mary's Street, had no windows (now, as the Factory Shop, it still hasn't) and the lights seemed to be on permanently. Mr Hart, a gentle and patient man, was the manager.

My favourite shop? Well it has to be the one next door to the Co-op, Spashett's toy shop and stationers. That was the shop window we children lingered at the longest, not on the way to school as we were usually in a hurry, but on the way home. That window was an Aladdin's Cave to us - in there were the Dinky toys we craved, or the next Famous Five book by Enid Blyton, or the set of crayons. And for the girls no doubt the latest doll, or doll's house or skipping rope. And as we gazed longingly into that bright window as dusk fell we would do our sums in our head, to try to work out how many weeks it would take to save up enough money for the latest Dinky toy (they were about 4s), or Famous Five novel (7s 6d). To our weekly pocket money we could add the possibility of a money prize in the Uncle Jack's Corner competitions in the Beccles and Bungay Journal - 7s 6d or 5s in the senior competition, and 5s or 2s 6d in the junior section.

Matchbox toys came in during the 1950s too - I seem to remember I bought the very first in the series, a dumper truck (or was it a road roller?).

In those days Sid and Dinky Payne lived in the house next to Spashett's and on the other side of them was Martin's the butchers (now Pex's fish and chip shop), then Whiteland's hardware, where you got such things as paraffin for lamps as well (he also did a regular delivery around the town) and then, beside the alley which now leads down to flats, was Johnson's woolshop. That was where we used to buy small skeins of rainbow wool with which to do tatting, making long multi-coloured snakes which we then sewed to form round table mats or other such useful things.

On the other side of that opening was Brown's watch and clock shop and jewellers - Mr Brown, who I remember as a white-

A Childhood Like Ours...

haired man with a large white moustache, used to make clocks, as well as repair them, and the shop was full of clocks of all kinds, from grandfather clocks to miniature timepieces.

Sturgess's shoe shop was next door to Brown's, selling all types of footwear. As with many shop owners in the town, the Sturgess's daughter, Pam, went to St Mary's School. The premises is now the Thai Restaurant. Then came the International Tea Company Stores - most towns of Bungay's size had a branch of that business in those days, and Mr Redden was the manager, with a large staff under him. When the business finally closed in the 1980s it became Londis, and is now a Spar shop.

Bowtell's ironmongers was next to that - one of those shops where you could get everything you needed for household repairs or making things - today it would be called a do-it-yourself store, but that phrase was not invented in the 1950s. It was a dark shop, and there was very little room when you went up the step inside, to be met by a long narrow counter, and behind that cabinets with drawers full of different sized nails, or screws, hinges, brackets or other such items, with each small drawer of the cabinet carefully marked.

There were other things on display - gardening implements, woodwork tools and so on - and if you wanted something not on show the assistants would disappear through a door behind the counter and find it.

It was a useful shop for Christmas presents for Dad, and next door was a shop useful for Christmas or Mothering Sunday presents for mum - Battell's crockery and chinaware shop, on the corner of the Fleece Hotel yard, run by Mr and Mrs Battell and also known as the East Suffolk Pottery Co. It sold a whole range of ornaments, flower vases, crockery and gifts, and you could go downs steps at the back of the shop and find another

A Childhood Like Ours…

section there.

All those four shops - Bowtell's is now Cooper's of Great Yarmouth and Battell's is another of Bungay's many hair salons - are in the ancient building which used to be Bungay's Guildhall in medieval times, and the first floor windowsills have some rare and ornate carvings which date back to the 16th or 17th century.

On the opposite corner of the Fleece yard entrance was Martin's pork butchers - the shop was an integral part of the Fleece building, was a butcher's shop until the early part of the 21st century, and has now been incorporated into the Fleece premises as a pool room. Mr Sutton, a former Town Reeve, ran that business.

Between the Fleece and the next shop is a large Regency building which had many office uses and during part of the 1950s served as the Labour Exchange. And next to it was Thirtle's millinery and haberdashery shop - another dark shop, deep and narrow, with the counter on the left-hand side as you went in. Mr Thirtle always seemed to wear a cloth cap, perhaps as an advertisement for the hats sold there, though they were mainly ladies headwear.

That premises is now a pharmacy - McDaniel's ran it as a chemists for many years after moving from Earsham Street, but at the time it was Thirtle's there was a chemist next door - a branch of Boots. That was where all the young mums went to have their babies regularly weighed to make sure they were growing steadily and healthily. The scales were in the public part of the shop, as were a set of scales for adults to weigh themselves - how many women would be seen weighing themselves in public today, whatever their size!

Boots the Chemist was the last shop in St Mary's Street, where Futter's Foodstore now operates, next to the entrance to Castle

A Childhood Like Ours...

Lane, with the Swan Inn on the other side. That ancient pub, which was there before the Great Fire of 1688, has changed little in outward appearance, though it is now trendily named Swanson's. Boots was also where you bought your cameras and films.

Into the Market Place, and on the north side of the Swan Inn Yard was Short's printers and stationers shop. Short's was one of the town's jobbing printers for the best part of a century, though I believe printing had ceased there before the 1950s, with the business concentrating on selling writing paper envelopes, pens, pencils, paints and other stationery items, some books, greetings cards, wrapping paper and similar items.

It was another shop I loved - there is something about that scent of fresh stationery and card. Miss Short, who ran it, sold Christmas cards loose, and we would rummage among them in a large tray, looking for the ones we wanted at 3d, or even less, each, and take them to the counter to be matched up with envelopes. It was there also that we bought boxes of paints - Reeve's paints, or Rowney's, in tin boxes, with each colour in its own white square tub neatly sunk into the contours of the tin.

Miss Short, with neat straight hair at neck length, always seemed to wear a brown skirt, with a brown cardigan over a white blouse, and her assistants wore similar uniform. She was a patient, gentle, attentive person, anxious to please, and my overriding recollection is of her saying, repetitively when serving you: "Yes, yes, yes...thank you, thank you," rather in the mode of Beatrix Potter's Jeremy Fisher when addressing Mrs Tittlemouse.

Next to Short's was Filby's menswear shop, another of those with a dark interior, and the suits, jackets and trousers on hangered racks round three sides, with shirts, vests and pants in drawers. That was where the bakery now is, and on the other

A Childhood Like Ours...

The Market Place, with Davey's wool shop, Reynold's Grocers and Gibson and Balls all clearly in view. Thirtle's millinery is the double-fronted premises at the back of the picture.

side of the covered opening next to it was Rowe's shoe shop, dark again, with boxes of shoes piled high on shelves on all sides. However, there was room for Mr Rowe to display, in a glass case mounted high on the wall, a fine specimen of a pike, which fascinated all young boys who went into the shop.

That shop has changed uses several times in the years since then, and is currently a ladies' fashion shop. Next to that was the Midland Bank, where Mr Tom Wortley was manager, and then came the original Chocolate Box - another shop we enjoyed going into to buy sweets or Mars bars, or ice-creams in the summer, with our pocket money. Grey's opticians now occupies those premises, and then came one of Bungay's main shops in those days, Gibson and Balls, grocers and ironmongers.

A Childhood Like Ours...

That large business occupied what is now the Chocolate Box - the grocery department - and Read's sports and menswear shop, the ironmongery department (Read's recently closed and is now Hobbyhorse). The latter was, as it is now, a deep narrow shop which sold the whole range of ironmongery items as well as animal traps and other rural equipment not regularly sold these days. It was Gibson and Balls who, in 1923, donated the Bungay Charity Cup, a fine piece of silverware still regularly competed for between local teams at the end of each season, raising money for charity and good causes in the process.

It was not until I got to the Market Place, on my journey to school, that I saw any shops on the other side of the street. Clockwise around the southern section of the Market Place were Reynold's grocer's shop (where the Norwich and Peterborough Building Society office now is), Ellen Cousten's haberdashery shop, a greengrocer's shop (now run by Alex Sprake), Ronnie Buck's fish shop, Warnes corn chandlery and animal feed business and, on the corner of St Mary's Street on that side, the electricity shop where you paid your electricity bill and could buy a whole range of electrical items.

In the northern section of the Market Place there was a café (Alfo's Café) where Abbott's estate agents now is - the Post Office was there up to 1930 - Lloyd's Bank was on the opposite side of the Bridge Street entrance, and Wightman's furniture and furnishings store was where it still is and has been since early in the 1800s. Davey's wool and sewing shop was also on that side of the Market Place - that was where you waited for the 11B bus to Norwich in those days, and if you wanted to put a parcel on the bus for transport, you left it at Davey's.

But my trip to school kept me on the west side of the Market Place and into Earsham Street, where the King's Head Hotel and the Three Tuns Hotel have stood for centuries on either side of

A Childhood Like Ours...

the entrance to that street. The King's Head was certainly Bungay's premier hotel in those days, with the town's main social and civic functions held there, and many wedding receptions and other events.

On the opposite corner of the entrance to the King's Head yard was Stead and Simpson's shoe shop - where, famously, shop assistant Gwen Honeywood found a message in a Wellington boot put there by one of the packers in the factory in far away Canada. She wrote back to that packer, Peter Ganci, a pen-friendship was established, and it led to Peter coming to Bungay to meet Gwen. They fell in love and were married in the town amid great press and television publicity, to complete a happy love story. They made their home in Bungay. Sadly, both have now passed on.

Each shop has its own aroma, of course - and none more so than Smith's tobacconists and seed shop, which was where Waveney Homes estate agents now is. The strong smell of tobacco of many varieties, mixed with the earthy scent of bulbs and seeds, was overpowering when you went through the door - it was relaxing, warm and comfortable.

Fowler's coal office was next to that as I moved along Earsham Street, past Whyte's sweet shop. Jars of mouth-watering goods filled the shelves - barley sugar, sherbert lemons, toffees, pear drops, pineapple chunks, spearmint chews, eucalyptus and others; and packets of fruit gums, chocolate bars and other confections filled racks on the counter. Later in the 1950s old Mr Whyte's son, Herbert, moved his newsagents shop from Broad Street into that premises and expanded it to incorporate both businesses. Crock's gift shop now occupies the site.

Another favourite shop for children in those days was The Bazaar, run by Mr and Mrs Plews, where the Earsham Street Café now offers haute cuisine. That was a shop for sweets and

A Childhood Like Ours…

toys and cards and ice-cream and all sorts of other things - and it was where I saw my first FA Cup game on television. There were still not too many of them about in those days, and Dad organised for me to watch Manchester City v Newcastle Utd. It was black and white, but as Newcastle played in black and white it didn't matter too much I suppose.

Earsham Street was a great place in the 1950s - next along was yet another sweet shop - the Mint House, opened by Leonard White and his wife in 1952 in premises which used to be a photographic shop. For pupils at St Mary's School, only around 100 yards away from that point, it became their tuck shop. Shelves were lined with jars of delicious looking sweets, liquorice sticks and barley sugar sticks and the counter with chocolate bars and goodies of all kinds. We would buy sweets in two-ounce portions at 3d each, so we got two lots for 6d. They loved having the children in, and Mr White continued to run the shop there for over 50 years, until he died in 2004, aged 84. It was one of the last traditional sweet shops in the area.

Eastaugh's bakery shop was a little further along, with another mouth-watering window to enjoy, with its cream and jam doughnuts, cream horns, coconut whirls, sponge cakes et al. There was a loke next to it, and on the opposite side of its entrance was Bingham's butchery, where Mum bought most of her meat. I remember the sawdust on the floor, the large metal hooks with joints or chickens or half pigs hanging from them, and the wooden slab, pitted with axe marks, on which joints and chops and sausages were cut to order. Mr Bingham was quite a fierce-looking man to us children, and he did not endear himself to me one day when our dog, Binky, who often accompanied us to school and then went back home on his own, went behind that wooden counter and he slapped him with his meat cleaver - fortunately with the flat of it. It probably scared us more than

A Childhood Like Ours...

Binky.

On we go, past Norman's shoe shop – Booty's later took the shop next door when Mr Booty, a man with a pronounced stoop, moved his wireless and electrical business there from Broad Street. I got my first pop record there - a 78rpm disc of Marion Ryan singing Mr Wonderful! I remember the words of that smoochy number to this day! Then we passed the White Lion pub - now the Castle Inn. In the yard in those days was a building which was the St John Ambulance Brigade headquarters, where later we played table tennis in the Bungay and District League for the Young Conservatives. On the other side of that entrance was Griffin's greengrocery shop, then a private residence, with the next shop being Butler's Fish and Chip shop, run by Cliff Butler and his wife. There used to be huge queues there, particularly on a Friday lunch time. The Butler's three children, Maureen, Stephen and Geoffrey, all went to St Mary's School It is still a fish and chip shop today, though with different owners of course.

That shop was next door to the Co-op grocery and butchery shop. It seemed a huge place in those days, taking up the whole area now occupied by Black Dog Antiques. No self-service then of course - you went round to each counter to ask for what you wanted, and we tended to go anti-clockwise, to the butchery first, then the cheese counter, and then the general groceries, which were on the left hand side of the building as you face it. At one time the butchery was in a separate building at the back, now the garage for the Belcher's house.

It was there that we had to cross the street to get to school. Every morning, without fail, Mum would say as she said goodbye: "Have you got a clean hanky? And remember to cross at the Vicarage (in Upper Olland Street) and at the Post Office."

Rumsby's iron foundry was adjacent to the Co-op on the same

A Childhood Like Ours…

side, though there was no shop premises as there is today, currently occupied by a bathroom accessories business.

And so we arrived at St Mary's School, Linden House, by the lime trees which stood (and still stand) on the outside of the path there. It had a beautiful garden, dominated by two large copper beech trees, under which children played at morning break and lunch-time, though the older boys played in the playshed, which stood where the car park for St Mary's House now is in Outney Road…

But more of that later…

A Childhood Like Ours...

And more Shops

BUT let's go back, on the other side of Earsham Street to the one we came on, to look at other shops. The Post Office, built where the original grammar school once stood, is still there today, but next to that was Cox's grocery business, occupying the premises now used by Bell's of Suffolk and Motley's fair trade gift shop. The thing I remember most about that was the 1d bags of crisps they used to sell - small bits of crisp. Mum reckoned they were the sweepings from the crisp factory floor, and didn't really like us eating them. But they were delicious.

At what is now the sweet scented New Beginnings Florists the aromas were of a different kind in the 1950s - Charlish's garage operated from those premises and the smell of petrol and oil emanated from there. Cars were serviced - Morris 8s, Hillman 10s, Austin 12s and the like were those which drew up there, unworried by any parking restrictions, to be served with petrol - just one sort - at around 3s a gallon. Sometimes they would need to be cranked from the front of the bonnet to get them going again. Mechanics were called upon only to serve the petrol, but it was only occasional work, in those days when self-service had not been thought of.

Charlish's Garage now operates from Bardolph Road of course, and next to it in its Earsham Street days was McDaniel's the chemists, where you went for your medicines and soaps and toiletries and various health aids such as liver salts and syrup of figs. Later McDaniel's moved to St Mary's Street – today it is the modern Boots.

On the east corner of Chaucer Street, where Phil Burton

A Childhood Like Ours…

Earsham Street in the 1950s, with Whyte's sweet shop on the left

Photography has recently moved in to replace The Greenhouse gift shop, was Trett's men's barber's shop, where as well as getting your short back and sides, the talk was of numbers one, or two or three - no, not the modern style of haircut but where the horses finished in the day's racing. Or it might have been of fishing - angling equipment was also sold there.

Further along Earsham Street what was once the Provincial Bank was the Labour Exchange in the 1950s, and two doors along, down three steps where Four Seasons ladies fashion shop is now installed, ladies went to Mrs Cator's hair salon for their cuts and bobs and curls and rinses.

Earsham Street House, now flats, was the Bungay Urban District Council offices, and beyond Cork Bricks there were private houses until you came to yet another grocer's and hardware store - Haward and Dawson. It occupied the premises now used by Howard's estate agents and Amor's Florists.

Today, next door to that, you could, until recently, buy toy cars.

A Childhood Like Ours...

This is the Festival of Britain parade through Bungay in June-July, 1951 as it passes through St Mary's Street, with the churchyard in the background. Bob Brock is the man smoking the pipe on the float.

A Childhood Like Ours…

In the 1950s those premises dealt with the real thing - T Simons Garage and petrol station was there, with the petrol pump hose stretching over the pavement to reach cars parked for fuel. We were always fascinated by the sight at the top of the hose where it joined the fixed overhead arm - there was a small glass section in which you could see the petrol as it flowed through. A 10s note might be tendered for the petrol, and probably 3s or 4s given in change.

Simon's garage was partly under what is the ballroom of The Three Tuns - dinners and dances and other functions were held there regularly in those days.

And so the memories of my trip to school are complete, but there were other shops in Bungay in those days which I didn't pass - Booty's when it was in Broad Street, where the off-licence at the top of Brandy Lane was Hunter and Oliver's.

Eastaugh's also had a baker's shop in Broad Street opposite the Horse and Groom (now the Green Dragon).

There was the Mayfair Cinema in that street (more of that elsewhere), Whyte's newsagents before it moved to Earsham Street, with Les Beckett's men's hairdresser moving in to replace it. Page' shoe repair shop was in that street too, next door to the Bungay Laundry - now of course the resurgent Fisher Theatre. And so to the café on the corner of Broad Street and Market Place.

Bridge Street led northwards from the Market Place, down to the river and over into Ditchingham. It was the route taken by the bus to Norwich, and some Beccles services went that way too. In Bridge Street, on the left going down, was Knights' men hairdressers, and Buckham's greengrocer shop, then The Chequers Inn, and beyond that Coe's grocery shop. On the right-hand side was Tucker's sweet shop (now the Red Shed), there was a fish and chip shop where Ronnie Buck's place now is, and

31

A Childhood Like Ours…

further down, just past the entrance to what was the vet's, was Denny's grocery shop, now a private house. Again, the Denny girls, Maureen and Berice, went to St Mary's.

In Lower Olland Street, before the Wharton Street car park was built, there was little Miss Rumsby's shop - small and dark, where you seemed to be able to get anything you could not get elsewhere in Bungay. And down past the fire station, with its air raid siren sounding to summon the men to a fire call, was Miss Raven's sweet shop. That was the tuck shop for the grammar school boarding house further down the street, and it sold ice-cream she made herself. That was also where Dad bought us our first chewing gum - Beechnut.

In Southend Road, on the corner of Flixton Road, was the general store and post office then run by Cyril and Beryl Bridges. Living in Southend Road, we always went there at least twice a week - on Tuesdays to draw the family allowance and get the groceries to last till Saturday, and on Saturday to spend our pocket money on sweets there. They were a lovely, friendly couple - years after they left, and even occasionally today, in our family we still refer to the shop simply as Bridges' though it is now a cycle shop – the sub-post office that was for years part of the grocery shop closed just a year ago. Watching Cyril cutting the cheese with a wire, or slicing ham on the manual slicer, was something I could never take my eyes off.

Another memory of Bridges: we bought Mansion Guardshine polish there, and one year you could collect a stamp from each tin, and once you got the full set (12 I think) you got a book of Cinderella with a pair of 3-D glasses. They allowed you to see the pictures in 3-D, something unknown to us then. The wait to get that 12th stamp seemed never-ending - but when I finally got it, to a small boy it was the realisation of a dream! At that age, the result was magical and wondrous.

A Childhood Like Ours…

Elsewhere there was a butcher's shop in Wingfield Street - now John Groom's - and Inwards' bakery had a branch at Annis Hill, as did the Co-op - the latter closed relatively recently.
Throughout the 1950s, and for many years after, PFK Ling's cycle shop was in Trinity Street, beside Borough Well Lane. And on the apex of the triangle between Upper and Lower Olland streets was Emery's radio and electricial shop – the first in Bungay to sell television sets. I remember seeing through the window a Test match being played on it. Emery's later moved into the Market Place.
That was about it. Today the town centre is much changed as far as its shops are concerned, and some seem to change hands quite frequently. But despite that, Bungay has changed little architecturally in the past century and a half - you only have to look at the roof lines to realise that and compare them with old pictures of the town. And it is that that helps it to retain its historic and traditional character and atmosphere.

A Childhood Like Ours...

The Mayfair Cinema

WALK along Broad Street in Bungay and you will come to Saxon Place - a modern town house development flush with the street line. That site is the last vestige of that house of adventure, escapism, romance, drama, excitement. The Mayfair Cinema.
Built in 1937 - to replace the New Cinema which was just down the street in what was, and now is triumphantly again, the Fisher Theatre - it was in its heyday in the early 1950s, when Technicolor was still new and many films were still in black and white.
I can't quite remember the first film I saw there as a young boy - it might have been *The Robe*, starring Richard Burton, or *Samson and Delilah*, starring Victor Mature and Jane Russell. Both were Biblical epics and I saw them both there at an early age. As a pupil at St Mary's School I remember we were taken to the Mayfair on two occasions - to see *Where no Vultures Fly*, a documentary about Africa, and *Flight of the White Heron,* another documentary about the Queen's first tour abroad, to Canada I believe, after succeeding to the throne.
That was 1953 - the same year, I'm certain, that long queues formed outside to see the film *The Dambusters*. They tailed round into the car park from the steps up to the Mayfair entrance, a rather grand entrance, which set it apart from cinemas in many other market towns in the area. They led into the foyer and the ticket office, with the walls adorned with posters of forthcoming attractions, and of the actresses and actors starring in them. The projection room was through a door on the right, and occasionally you would catch a glimpse, if

A Childhood Like Ours…

manager Mr Phelps was just coming in or out, of what seemed huge reels turning on the projector.

The ticket office was on the left of the foyer, with programmes available, packets of sweets on the adjoining counter, and tickets served through an opening in a shiny metal surface. The entrance to the auditorium was directly opposite the entrance, and in those days usherettes in uniform, and carrying torches, were there to show you to your seat. At the interval between films - there was always a main film and a B film (the word movie had not crossed the Atlantic from the USA in those days) - the usherettes would become sales girls, offering ice-creams and lollipops from trays held by straps around their necks. Emergency exits were at the front, at floor level on either side of the screen, the one on the left hand side leading out into the car park.

Watching films there was a wondrous experience at that age, when Technicolor was still new. And there was a thriving Saturday morning children's club. There was a main film, often a cowboy feature, a cartoon, trailers, and a serial. *Flash Gordon* was a popular one, and there were also cowboy serials. Whichever they were, they ended each week with the hero in situations it seemed impossible to survive. You HAD to return next week to see what happened - and of course, the hero survived.

Those Saturday mornings were noisy affairs, with the heroes being loudly cheered and the baddies booed, rather in pantomime style, with the manager often having to call for quiet. And birthdays were marked with the presentation of a packet of sweets at the front of the cinema before the film started.

The adverts on the screen were all part of the entertainment - many of them advertising local shops and garages, others advertising national merchandise, such as cars. One that sticks most clearly in my mind was for a car I coveted, even at the age of 14 or 15. It was the Renault Dauphine. I knew nothing about the workings of cars, but it had such beautiful smooth lines, with no angles, and the one advertised was sky blue in colour. It purred quietly along the road, and I fell in love with it and never grew tired of seeing that advert. But I never did get to own that svelte-like automobile.

In the early 1950s, films were given two main certificates - U or A. With A films you had to be accompanied by an adult to get in if you were under 14, and sometimes I would wait outside for an adult to come along and ask them to "get me in" - which they usually did. Those A certificates signified that some scenes were a bit too realistic, but truth to tell they were tame indeed compared with the graphic realism you can see in films and on television today. Towards the middle of the 1950s X certificates were brought in, mainly for features such as the Hammer horror films - Dracula, Frankenstein, and others with titles such as *The Pit and the Pendulum*. They seemed pretty scary then - today's children would not blink an eyelid.

But the Mayfair in the 1950s was a great amenity for Bungay, with films changing twice a week. They were days when the early evening programme finished at around 8.10pm (the main film was shown for a second time after that, and you could sit through it twice if you wanted to), and you went out into the cool dusk, with the pavements maybe dampened by a shower, and galloped home, pretending to be on the steed of your cowboy hero, and forming your hand into a six-shooter to aim at imaginary Indians as you made your way home.

Maybe you would stop at the fish and chip shop for three-pennorth of chips, though we were forbidden to eat them in the street on the way home.

A Childhood Like Ours…

They were good days with good memories of the harmless escapism the Mayfair provided. It was a sad day indeed when it finally closed in the 1990s.
But, as with those big reels on the old projectors, wheels turn full circle. Today, films are now being shown again in Bungay, at the re-opened Fisher Theatre - the venue where the first films were shown in Bungay 90 years ago…

A Childhood Like Ours…

Bungay Grammar School

I STOPPED at the gates, and looked up the drive to the building ahead. The clock on its gable front was stopped at 8.55am, the row of lime trees on either side stood sentinel to anyone going up that drive, now unkempt and overgrown, as they had done for more than 75 years since the building was built and opened in 1925.

And suddenly the scene changed, and I was back in September, 1954, at that same spot - only the drive was neatly gravelled, with no weed in sight, the edge of the well trimmed playing fields making a straight line on either side, and the wide green bobs of the lime trees immaculate atop their grey trunks. The goalposts were up on the pitches on either side of the drive too, ready for the football season.

It was my first day at Bungay Grammar School, and I began my first walk up that drive - a trip I was to make on hundreds of occasions in the next six years, clad in black blazer with school badge on the pocket, black and white slant-striped tie on shirt, and cap with tiny badge on head. The clock said 8.55am but it was not stopped, and I was soon among others hurrying up the drive for school to start at 9am.

Bungay Grammar School was a boys only school in those days, housed in a single storey building with a central corridor running from one end to the other, accessed by wooden double doors at either end. From the northern end, the cloakroom was immediately on the left as you entered - lines of pegs on which to hang your coat and satchel and stow your sports kit underneath. A line of hand basins with only cold water, and a cupboard down one side with a variety of kit and equipment in

A Childhood Like Ours...

it.

Those hand basins were the site of the traditional induction ritual to which all new pupils in the first year were subjected - being chased around the field by second year pupils, caught and dragged into that cloakroom to be ducked under those cold water taps.

It wasn't a brutal rite and I got through it quite happily, and found my two colleagues who had also moved up from St Mary's School, Jonathan Wortley and Graham Button. We knew our way around - there had been an introduction afternoon the day before, when we were shown the six classrooms down one side - three of them, rooms three, four and five, doubled as the school hall, with folding partitions drawn back for the conversion every morning for school assembly - and on the other side the woodwork room, store room, sixth form room, headmaster's study, the library, staff room, with staff toilet behind, and the science laboratory. Pupils toilets were outside, behind the cycle sheds.

Staff stayed in their dedicated classrooms - pupils moved from room to room, up and down the central corridor, according to their time-table. When I started there Leslie (Java) Jolly taught geography and Religious Instruction (and ran an after-school stamp club) in room one, Tom Spode taught French in room two, Harold (Plug) Goundry taught Maths in room three, Frank (Dukes) Hadingham taught English in room four, Fanny Houghton taught art in room five (as the only woman member of staff, we were required to call her Sir, in line with the others), and Don Houghton taught history in room six, where headmaster Douglas (Scruff) Hewitt also taught Latin.

Some sixth form tuition - the sixth form was small, probably no more than 20 in all stayed on after taking GCE O-levels) - often took place in the sixth form common room or the library. Smiler

A Childhood Like Ours...

Thomas taught woodwork and Peter Howard taught science, though Gig Powell was there when I started.

The cane was the normal form of punishment in those days. If you were sent out of a class for mucking around, you stood outside the door, and if Scruff Hewitt came out of his room and saw you, you would be for the cane. He would summon you to his room, select his cane (he had a number, from a short whippy one to a long bamboo cane with a split end which was certainly the most painful to receive), order you to bend over - "Bend over I say! Touch your toes - touch your toes I say."

Then: "Whack!" You would feel the searing pain, your eyes would water and you would be dismissed back to your lesson. Sometimes of course, you would receive more than one stroke, depending on the nature of the misdemeanour - the most I received at any one time was three, and you knew you had been caned!

In my school career, I kept count of the strokes of the cane I had - 32 in all. But I can't say it scarred me psychologically in any way, and I would always defend it as an appropriate form of punishment. It hurt, but it was much quicker than writing a hundred lines repetitively - "I must not talk in class."

I enjoyed school, especially sport and PT, which provided the chance to get out on to the school field. Sitting in the classroom during the lesson before games, I found it difficult to concentrate, having one eye on the weather outside, hoping against hope that it would not rain. If it did, games were cancelled and you stayed in doing lessons - there was no such luxury as an indoor gym to do sport in.

And yet I loved the yearly exams - the whole atmosphere of them. Sitting in the classroom in the summer with the windows open, the scent of the newly mown grass on the school field wafted through the open window into the perfectly quiet room, mingling with the contrasting scent of fresh paper on which the questions had been roneoed, probably the night before. There was something very peaceful and relaxing about it. I was not necessarily good at all the subjects - certainly not maths or science - but I enjoyed the physical act of putting pen to paper and seeing the ink forming words there. I always have, and still do, even in these days of computers. In some ways the satisfaction is the same - seeing the words forming on the screen and creating something to read. Handwriting was the only option for a teenager, anyway, in the 1950s.

The wartime aid raid shelters were still on - or under- the school field, at an area which came to be known as The Oval. That was where fights would take place to settle any schoolboy argument. The word would go round the school at lunch-time or morning break - "There's a fight up the Oval!" Boys would flock there to witness it, until they and the combatants were dispersed by one of the masters. They were never serious fisticuffs, certainly not in my time there, and as far as I know no injuries.

House matches - football in the winter term, hockey in the spring term and cricket in the summer term - were always played after school (school ended at 3.45pm), with 15 minutes each way, with juniors on the pitch to the left of the drive going up, and seniors to the right - the same went for Under 15 and senior matches against other schools, which were played on Saturday mornings. In those days we played Sir John Leman Grammar School at Beccles, Leiston Grammar, Diss Grammar, City of Norwich School, Lowestoft Grammar, Yarmouth Grammar and Thorpe Grammar. The Under 15s also had games against Bungay Secondary Modern School.

We won some and lost some, with the keenest battles being against the Sir John Leman.

There was a religious assembly every morning. We stood up as

A Childhood Like Ours…

Mr Hewitt and the staff, their gowns flowing behind them, marched in to take their places, and then all the boys sat on the floor, between the desks, to be required to listen to a piece of classical music, relayed into the hall from the record player in the library. Sitting on that dusty floor was not the ideal way to be educated into the beauties of classical music, but I remember one or two pieces, particularly the 1812 Overture, and Trumpet Voluntary.

Then we would have a hymn - with Tom Spode at the piano, although sometimes a classmate of mine, David Storey, would be deputed to the task - and a reading. Again, only one or two stick in my mind today, perhaps because they came round every term or so, on a rota basis. There was one, written by the Russian emperor Tolstoy writing 2000 years before Christ, and another from Shaw's play St Joan.

The particular phrase I remember from that one is St Joan saying as her inquisition: "You tell me I am alone. But France is alone, and God is alone, and what is my loneliness to that of my country and my God."

Mr Hewitt always read those passages, and then there were prayers and dismissal. Except on Friday mornings, when we had hymn practice, to learn a new hymn. Again it was led by the headmaster, who would loudly call out "Breath!" when we had to fill our lungs in advance of two or three lines which did not allow time to breathe.

Play time would be spent out on the asphalt, with teams of about 20 or more kicking a tennis ball around. At dinner time - the midday meal was called that in those days - I always went home to dinner, but usually came back as quickly as I could to join the kick around.

It meant another trip up the drive along the avenue of limes, through the middle of the expansive school field. In those days,

A Childhood Like Ours…

to the back of the school, was the field covered with logs, put there for seasoning by Edgar Watts, who had a factory in Southend Road making wefts for cricket bats. Bats that began their life in that sawmill were used by many of the top Test batsmen of the day to score famous centuries on grounds in this country and around the world.

Today the school field is much changed. There was no fire station - the school garden, run by Java Jolly, was where that now stands - no skateboard park, no Adele House nursing home (one goal of the first team pitch, and the old cricket pavilion, was where that stands now), no Bungay Medical Centre, and no houses on the north or south side the school. And the old 1925 school building is now converted to flats, and the school canteen to the youth club.

But the avenue of limes, and the school clock, continue to evoke happy memories of a school that I loved and enjoyed, and where I was proud to be a pupil…

A Childhood Like Ours…

St Mary's School

AT the end of Earsham Street, on the corner of Outney Road, there are twin stone gateposts, leading into a short walk to the steps of the big Georgian house.
On one is engraved Linden House. On the other, St Mary's School.
They are the only reminders today of the private school which was based in Linden House for more than 70 years, till it closed in 1966. In the late 1940s and early 1950s it was where I and my brothers and sister spent our first years of learning.
It was at its height then. The board outside the school announced: *St Mary's School for Girls- Preparatory for Boys,* and 180 boys and girls enjoyed their days there, under the care and guidance of joint principals Miss K Doble and Miss M F Mawdesley, and two other staff for whom school was their home, Miss C Ridout and Miss E Peatman.
It was their home and we were their children. I'm sure they loved us as their own, and they dedicated their lives to giving us a good grounding in basics subjects, but also in good manners, respect for elders, tidiness.
On the time table were such subjects as nature, dictation, composition, writing (yes, great emphasis was put on how to form joined up writing properly), reading, French, history, geography, and sums (for the girls who stayed beyond the 11+ age it became mathematics).
We walked to school. Those who came from outlying areas (they came from as far away as Saxmundham and Trowse to St Mary's) arrived by car and taxi, or walked from the bus stop, and all entered the school by the door just into Outney Road, up

A Childhood Like Ours...

two steps. Those who biked went in at an entrance from Scales Street. And at the end of the day Miss Stansby would stand on that front step and call your name when your parents or transport arrived. "Loddon taxi No 1!" or "Loddon taxi No 2!" was her familiar cry.

Once inside you went up four steps and into the lobby which led through to the teachers' study and the school hall, where everyone assembled each morning for a hymn, prayers, and announcements. During the summer when exams were on, the results of each subject, form by form, would be read out to everyone by Miss Mawdesley, standing on a bench in her blue tweed suit and brown socks so she could be clearly seen.

She would start at the top, with the marks always out of 100: "History: First John Jones 97, second Jill Smith 95, third Tom Carter 91..." and so on. When the marks got down to 50, that was the cut off point and that was emphasised: "...James Wilson 50. The others failed: Brenda Barker 48, Christine Ford 45..."

It was unequivocal - if you got below 50 marks you had failed and needed to do better, and you knew where you stood. There was no banning of the word failure in those days.

The school hall doubled as the dining-room, and was dominated by the curved staircase with polished rail and bannister leading up to the first floor, though they were for private use, not the children. On one side of the hall, a stained glass window looked into the fourth and fifth form room, and a short, curving corridor led into forms 2A and 2B.

They were in a large, high-ceilinged room, with a bay window looking out on to the beautiful garden, which was also the playground. It was dominated by two large copper beech trees, and a central, immaculate lawn. We were only allowed on the lawn for the annual school photograph, or the annual displays in which each form presented an item. For us boys it was PT drill for which we were coached by Miss Mawdesley in the play shed. That was a large wooden floored shed bordering Outney Road on one side, with the other side open and bordered by the crinkle-crankle wall dividing it from the garden.

Miss Mawdesley was proud of her boys and how she trained them. There was a well at one end of the shed with a raised stone cover, and she would stand on that directing operations: "Astride, together - lunge, together - astride, together - lunge, together! Halt! At ease!"

She could easily have been a sergeant major in a previous life!

Boys played football or cricket in that shed at break and lunchtimes, or marbles in season. The girls played in the garden - a popular game was releases (called tag elsewhere I believe), or making houses, or just walking around the beautiful, typically English garden, full of flowers at all times - snowdrops and aconites in winter, crocuses, primroses, wallflowers, daffodils, and bluebells in spring, hollyhocks, Canterbury bells, honeysuckle, orange blossom, roses and many others, and many shrubs, in the summer. There were two air raid shelters in the garden we were not allowed in, but that did not stop us occasionally venturing in.

The whole garden was surrounded by a high brick wall, and it was an idyllic location, conducive to learning. But we were not confined there - Miss Ridout would take us on nature walks on the Common, Earsham Dam and elsewhere to look and learn about flowers and wildlife, and the common was also our sports field. The girls played hockey there on a pitch in front of the golf clubhouse, and the boys would play football on the same pitch - using hockey sized goals of course. And it was at the same location that the annual sports day would take place - we would march from the school along Outney Road and over the bridge over the railway line for the afternoon. It was always

A Childhood Like Ours…

high summer and always hot and sultry, with the grass browned by the sun - at least that is what memory tells me, but no doubt there were years when it was rained off.

There would be running races, high jump, bean bag races, three-legged races and so on, with parents sitting in their chairs or deck chairs, or on blankets on the ground, to watch. I loved those days, though I never won - the nearest I came was third, with Jonathan Wortley and Graham Button always beating me. The old Waveney Valley line was still busy then, and sometimes the train driver would sound his steam whistle in greeting when he saw the activity there.

At St Mary's, life started at five years old, in Kindergarten, which was on the first floor in an extension room, adjoining the room used as division one and division two. We learnt sums with counters and about money with cardboard coins, and we were taught French from that stage too. Miss Peatman would command us in turn to "Touchez la table," "Touchez la fenetre," or "touchez le nez," and we would do it in turn.

In history we learned about pre-historic man in division two I remember, through stories about Sharpe-Eye and his family, and Sabretooth the Tiger. In handwork we cut out the felt shapes of a dog or a cat, sewed them together with blanket stitch, and stuffed them to fill them out before putting in the final stitches.

Much is said about recycling as a modern thing these days. At St Mary's we were recycling in the early 1950s (I was there till 1954). At Christmas used exercise books would be cut into strips, we would colour them with crayons all the colours of the rainbow, and paste the strips into paper chains which we hung up to decorate the room, supplementing bought paper trimmings, in the shape of bells and balls. And we were taught about the Christmas story in the cosy afternoons before the roaring open fire which heated those rooms.

A Childhood Like Ours...

Other classrooms elsewhere in the school were heated by coke boilers - turtle stoves they are sometimes called - though transition, up a short flight of steps outside division one, had an open fire too. The boilers were in form one, which was on the first floor of a separate block on the corner of Scales Street, above form three, and in that classroom too. When they were working well they were very effective, but sometimes they would smoke terribly, and smell, and we would all be coughing and spluttering. What today's modern health and safety officials would have made of them I don't know, but we came to no harm.

Coke boilers also heated form two, and the fourth and fifth form room.

Christmas concerts were held in the Chaucer Institute, just along the road in Popson Street. The younger children would perform their well rehearsed singing games, Miss Mawdesley's drill team would go through their routines on stage, the older girls would sing chorally, and there would also be a fully costumed play, often Shakespeare, performed by the oldest girls in the school, coached by Miss Iris Castle, with Miss Oldham (who always arrived at the school on a sit-up-and-beg cycle with stringed mudguards) providing piano accompaniment where necessary.

My recollection is that school was always stimulating and always enjoyable in those halcyon days of the early fifties when life was returning to normal after the second world war. We were blessed with dedicated teachers and the lack of modern diversions such as television, computers and ipods. And most of us thrived on it, though as in every generation, there were those who hated school and were unhappy there.

Today, St Mary's School is St Mary's House residential home for the elderly - much changed internally and its residents at the

A Childhood Like Ours…

other end of the age scale. But though the magnificent main copper beech, and the playshed and air raid shelters have gone, there are glimpses of the old school to be seen there still.
For the residents who ended their days there after being pupils in another age the memories must have been sweet and soulful…

There were other schools in Bungay of course - Bungay Primary School in Wingfield Street, where it was established in 1877 as the National Board School, St Edmund's Roman Catholic Primary School, opened in St Mary's Street in the 1890s, and the secondary modern school in Hillside Road East (now the middle school), built as the area school in 1939, as well as the grammar school already mentioned. Children would have had their own memories, hopefully mainly fond ones, of their days there, their teachers, their friends and their surroundings. In the 1950s, nearly 1000 pupils in all would have been at the five schools at any one time…

A Childhood Like Ours…

This is another picture of the Festival of Britain Parade through Bungay in 1950. It is moving through Broad Street.

A Childhood Like Ours…

Stow Fen and Outney Common

RIVERS and open spaces were where we had our adventures and activities in the 1950s - out in the open air under the sun, or in the wind, or sometimes in the rain or snow. If we had to stay indoors we found plenty to do - writing stories, drawing, reading, inventing games with our toys. Looking back, it was we who were lucky and privileged, not today's children who sit in front of television sets, or computers, or play stations and "enjoy" repetitive and often violent games. My optimistic belief is that they are still in the minority.

Stow Fen was one of those places we went to frequently in the holidays. I had a friend, Geoffrey Greenbank, who lived at Fen Farm, which backed on to the fen off Flixton Road, with his garden and fields giving access directly on to it.

We would go fishing at Earsham Mill in the spring, or at a number of points along the river there either side of it. We had very basic fishing rods - just a rod and reel, and line and hook - very often not even a quill, because we could see into the clear water where our bread bait was, and position it close to the fish which were also clearly visible. Dace, roach, gudgeon, perch and the occasional eel were what we caught mostly - not large specimens, but it was the satisfaction of feeling the tug on the line and lifting it out of the water, by the trees and bushes along the bank, and looking at it, and throwing it back in.

There was one spot on the fen, the furthest point towards Bungay, where the main river was joined by a stream, and there was a bridge across. We would fish from the bridge, looking down into the water, or across to a deeper spot under a shady tree. There were a number of perch there - the prettiest fish we ever caught, with their clear striped scales and prominent dorsal fin.

I caught the biggest fish I ever caught from that bridge. Leaning over, I could see it in the clear water, and dropped my line with its bait on near to it - and to my great joy and excitement it took it. Geoff's Dad happened to be there, and he helped me to land it, a fine specimen of a roach, weighing in at three-quarters of a pound - not huge by angling standards but to me it was a prize fish.

It made me late for dinner that day, but I proudly went into the kitchen, holding it up so mum could see - the only fish, I think, that I ever took home.

Dad would occasionally take me to fish there, by the mill, in the printing works summer holidays - in the 1950s, as was the custom at many factories throughout the country, the works closed for a fortnight, with everyone having the same holiday period. It was the only chance he got to do things like that with us, as he did all the overtime that was going to help make ends meet, so it was really special when he took me there. One of my abiding memories of him is standing there on the bank, with rod in hand, dangling a fish on the end of the line. It may only have been a 2oz dace, but it was a fish!

Every time I walk across Stow Fen these days, I see Dad there, still, in his sports jacket and grey flannels, and open-necked white shirt.

We swam in the river at Stow Fen too. Earsham Mill, where the mill stream joins the main river, was a popular spot, and on hot days in the summer holidays there would be 50-60 children there, some with parents and picnics. It had a sandy bottom, with deep and shallow spots, and was perfectly safe - not that we ever thought in terms of "safe" and "dangerous" in those

A Childhood Like Ours...

days, though perhaps parents at home did.

There was a spot further along, towards Bungay, where we swam on the fen too, though not so often, and it was at that spot that I finally could say I could swim, at least under water. The river was swollen by heavy rain and had that brown colour to it. There were only two of us, David Cobb and myself, and it was pretty cold. Maybe it was the added volume of water that helped, but I was elated when I found myself swimming under water in a controlled way for the first time!

Cattle grazed the fen of course, as they still do - a timeless use of meadows unaltered for centuries.

So it is on Outney Common, too - another favourite playground of the 1950s - more popular than Stow Fen, and I went swimming there much more often than the fen. Sandy was the place, where the Waveney separated the common from Ditchingham, and by a small, narrow island, on the eastern side of which was the artificial cut which gave access to the Mill House, once the home of George Baldry. He died in around 1960, and his home was later demolished, leaving only the foundations which can still just be discerned if you clear the undergrowth. Today, in late January and February, the site of the house is covered by a carpet of snowdrops.

At Sandy in the summer holidays up to 200 used to swim there, or laze on the grassy bank and sunbathe. There was a diving board on a tall tree at the end of the island which the braver boys - or maybe the show-offs - used to dive from. It was maybe 15ft from the surface of the water, but with the river probably 12ft deep below it, it was perfectly safe. The less adventurous swimmers contented themselves with swinging out on the rope which was attached to another chestnut tree on the island, and then letting go and plunging into the water - refreshing on hot days, cold on colder days. I remember the first time I went there it was a dull cold day. I couldn't swim, and Sandy Wortley pushed me in out of my depth. But I managed to grab the bank and haul myself out to safety, shivering with the momentary fear - and the cold.

At one time there was primitive changing accommodation there, erected by the Urban District Council, but it had disappeared by the time I began to go there regularly, and people got changed as best they could, with towels wrapped around their waist, standing self-consciously on the crowded bank.

One day, as I was changing, there was a girl standing in front of me, with her back to me, trying to change, and in the awkwardness of that operation her towel slipped, exposing her round pink bottom. No doubt I gawped and stared, and she glanced round in childish embarrassment, and said in her broad Suffolk accent: "Hev yer got an eyeful?"

She quickly pulled her towel up again to regain her modesty, while I, no doubt, went bright red with embarrassment. She is still around Bungay today - I wonder if she remembers the incident as clearly as I do!

The old river runs through the middle of the Lows on the Common, maybe 100 yards from the main Waveney - you cross it on the bridge as you approach Sandy from the Bungay direction though often we cycled there, over Ditchingham Dam and along the lane and over the iron bridge to Sandy from that direction.

The old river was often stagnant in the summer, and a favourite spot for cattle to drink and ruminate and flick away the flies on their faces. We called it the hot country, because under the hot sun the water was literally warm - if not hot. Running over to it and lying in it after coming out of the cold water of the flowing main river was a wonderful feeling, and we would lie and wallow there in the shallow, muddy and no doubt cattle clouded water. Health experts and hygienists would hold up their hands in horror today at such behaviour - but it did us no harm at all. We never caught anything, and maybe were even more healthy for exposing ourselves to it.

We'd take books to ready on the banks in the sun, with the trees on the island and the azure summer skies the backdrop to what was an idyllic part of our childhood.

Walking on the common was another activity - we would take the dogs there regularly, through the myriad of paths through the gorse, or around the river, weaving in and out of the bushes and undergrowth and walking in that beautifully soft species of grass that is at its peak in high summer.

One year, we made a camp in the gorse bushes, crawling into an open space below the green and gold, and sweeping the floor clear of gorse needles and rabbit droppings. We grabbed handfuls of that soft grass to use as a carpet for the camp, and there we would lie, with our picnic, or reading our books or just mucking around in the ways children did - happy, content, bothering no one, wrapped up in our adventure and play.

If memory serves me right that camp was on what is now the 18th fairway of the golf course - a huge area of gorse there was destroyed by the fire there in the late 1950s which caused considerable controversy in the town.

It also destroyed our beloved and carefully constructed camp in the gorse.

The common was - and is - a delight whatever the season. In spring when the skylarks and linnets were nesting in fern and gorse and blackberry; in summer for the reasons already mentioned, and when harebells danced in the breeze, and when we spent most time there; in autumn when we gathered blackberries, or fished in the lake or river; and in winter, when it was covered with snow and the lake froze, sometimes, and people played snowballs or took their toboggans to shoot down the slopes.

I remember one huge snowball fight on the common one year, after a particularly heavy fall of snow. Two groups lined up on either side of the plague pit and pounded each other with snowballs. The gap was quite wide between the sides at that point and many missiles fell short, but plenty found their targets too. It was an exhilarating, glowing, breathless battle which lasted over an hour and left our woollen gloves wet and hands numb with cold inside them, and we went home cold but exuberant to thaw out by a glowing coal fire.

Which side won the battle? It simply didn't matter. That really was one of those occasions when it was the taking part that counted for everything.

Many boys would go fishing on the Common in the 1950s, either in the river or in the lake - the large pond created when gravel was dug for the building of Flixton airfield during the war. As on the fen, we caught mainly dace, roach, perch and gudgeon, and the occasional small pike. Often we fished at Sandy, or Finches Well, opposite Ditchingham Lodge, but you could pick any point along the river there.

Throughout the first half of the fifties, regular point to point racing took place on the Common - the grandstands were still there, though somewhat dilapidated, and the fences in place, nine in all I believe around the course which took in much of the Common. We always had a day off school for the racing, and went along to enjoy the atmosphere and the crowds. It was an occasion eagerly looked forward to - we didn't know much about the races, and certainly didn't bet, but we tried to position ourselves near one of the jumps in the hope, I have to admit, of seeing a dramatic fall or other mishap. Some of the minor stakes

A Childhood Like Ours…

A goods train working in Bungay station in the 1950s, as mentioned in this chapter. One of those trains, perhaps, that children believed might drip boiling oil on to them in the river!

had very few runners, but the main races of the day had quite big fields, and the thunder of the hooves of a dozen horses as they approached the jumps, divots of turf flying from their feet as they did so, could be heard easily above the noise and cheers of the huge crowds which gathered for the Bungay races in May. It was a sad day when racing there finally came to an end in 1957. The main grandstand had been removed in 1953 and re-erected on the Maltings Meadow, to where Bungay Town moved their headquarters from Earsham Rec that year.

The Common was Bungay's back garden, enjoyed by many people. A favourite place for families was a shallow area by the golf club, known in the 1950s simply as The Train Bridge, because it was just by the spot where the Waveney Valley Line crossed the River Waveney and the trains slowed into Bungay Station. On hot summer afternoons mums would sit on the bank and chat and watch their children splash in the shallow water, or peer into the water trying to spot minnows, or try to catch them in their nets. The bottom was sandy and it was little more than a foot deep for the most part, though under the bridge there were deeper spots, perhaps three feet deep, and only the more adventurous children ventured there. Indeed, the popular gossip that went round among the children playing there was that "you shouldn't go under the bridge when a train comes in case boiling oil from it falls on you and burns you!"

That never happened of course - it was just one of those misconceptions that children had. But it was exciting when a train came across the bridge, hissing steam and, very often sounding its whistle as a greeting when the driver saw the children playing there.

It must have been a wonderful semi-rural scene in those days when there was no concern about playing or swimming in the river, and if you banged your foot or cut your toe on something,

A Childhood Like Ours…

a plaster would be put on it and back in you would go. It was a perfect picnic spot, close to the town - plenty of time for the families to get home in time for Mum to prepare tea for Dad when he came home from the printing works.

Go there today, and you find those scenes cannot be repeated. Vegetation has been allowed to grow up on the bank there, making access to the water difficult should families want to take their children there to paddle. The play equipment - swings, see-saw and climbing frame - is still there, but the attraction of the water and the chance to picnic on the grassy bank is gone.

Perhaps, one day, that idyllic activity will be made possible again…

A Childhood Like Ours...

The Side Gate

HAVE you ever thought how inanimate, ordinary, unnoticed objects we take for granted play a significant part in our lives - particularly our childhood?
It came home to me one day many years ago, when I returned to my childhood home in Southend Road, Bungay. The object was the side-gate - it suddenly wasn't there any more, and I mourned its passing in my mind almost as if I had lost an old friend, and realised how much a part it was of my childhood in the fifties. I wrote this in January, 1978:

THE dear old battered side gate had gone.
After nearly 40 years of standing up to the frequent comings and goings of people and animals, and after being regularly pounded by children, cricket bats, balls, pram wheels and bicycles, not to mention the natural elements of wind, rain and snow, it is there no more.
It is gone from it space beside the semi-detached house at Bungay. It seems strange, perhaps, that such an object as the side gate could be the subject of nostalgic memories, could command affection, even bring a sentimental lump to the throat.
Certainly it had not occurred to me that this was possible till one spring day when I visited my mother at her home, where I was brought up and lived for 20 years (and had visited frequently since) and saw that the side gate had gone.
In its place was a curly, tall wrought-iron gate, its thin, spaced uprights and curly bits painted blue and white and giving a clear view of the back garden beyond; a functional enough piece of garden furniture, but new, with no personality.
It wasn't the dear old Side Gate.

A Childhood Like Ours…

That old gate, you see, wasn't just a gate; it wasn't even A side gate - it was THE side gate, and was always referred to by all members of the family as that, ever since I can remember. It was part of the house and almost part of the family, and had been there for the past 40 years.

As I stood and pondered momentarily at its passing - yes, pondered sadly, even though the new gate was structurally, functionally and certainly aesthetically infinitely better than its dilapidated old predecessor - I realised how full my memories were of such a seemingly inanimate object, and its involvement in the family's (particularly the children's) activities.

In its way it probably provided a very real part of the security of a humble but happy home, in the same way as did The Birch Tree - a silver birch which stood at the end of the garden (just outside our garden boundary actually, and in Miss Wightman's) and was always referred to as The Birch Tree, as it stood there steadfastly through the seasons, heralding the changes of each through the years, through its leafy cloak of changing colours. It does so still.

The Side Gate was a wooden gate about five feet high, with a steel latch operated by a handle and thumb press from the outside. It separated the front garden from the back, giving access, from the front, to a concrete uncovered passageway about six feet wide, between the house and a corrugated iron fence which bordered the neighbouring garden at that point.

The passage - we always called it The Passage - was about ten yards long and gave access to the back door, the coalhouse and the outside lavatory. At the end of the kitchen wall it widened out into the back garden.

That passage may sound awfully small. I suppose it was, on reflection. But as children we played there for hours, in sunshine or snow, wind or rain. At various times it was our Wembley, our

A Childhood Like Ours...

Lords, or Wimbledon, a marble pitch, car track, bicycle repair yard, somewhere to make marks with bits of chalk you dug up in the garden...

It was there that my love of ball games was nurtured, and the Side Gate played an important part in that. It was the road end goal, and you would not believe the exciting football matches that took place there. The games I remember most were between me and Dad and my elder brother, Robin - me and Dad on one side. We played with a tennis ball, or one of those very bouncy rubber balls, and one of the dividing lines between the concrete slabs was the kick-off spot.

Dad was usually on my side but played a fairly static game, positioning himself by the bathroom window, and intercepting when necessary. We always seemed to kick into the Side Gate goal, and you had to hit the gate direct - hitting the gatepost did not count, not did a rebound onto the gate from the fence, or the side of the house. We played after tea usually, often till dusk, till the bats came out and the sun was setting behind the privet hedge at the bottom of the garden, and Mum called a halt by announcing that she had made the cocoa.

I remember one day Robin made a cup out of an old silver Bourneville cocoa tin, and we decided to play a cup final for it. It was a hectic game. Dad and me frequently scored by hitting the Side Gate goal, but then each side's score invariably ran into double figures in these games, and this one was no exception.

Finally, with dusk falling, we decided to play the first to 20. It must have been early summer, for I recall the high pitched twittering of swallows in the twilight as the game reached its climax. I was bitterly disappointed when my brother got the goal that meant he won 20-19, but looking back, Dad probably engineered it that way, as we had two players against one.

Mum came out and presented the cocoa tin cup to Robin, and

A Childhood Like Ours…

we all went in from the near darkness to the bright light of the kitchen, where we had a whole "long" of Kit-Kat as a reward for a fine game. That somewhat appeased my tired irritability at the result - Robin made the cup, so I suppose it was only right that he should win it.

The Side Gate also served as a cricket wicket - and very effective wicket-keeper. The stumps and bails were chalked on the woodwork. We only had one batsman, and the bowler bowled from the back garden end, at a point level with the end of the kitchen wall, and always underarm of course.

Many's the wicket that fell with the ball hitting the chalk marks on the side Gate, and many's the runs made from that position. An accurate straight drive to the far end of the garden was a four, and if you hit it over the fence into Mr Newham's garden next door, it was "six and out."

The ball went next door much more frequently at cricket than football, of course, and here, too, the Side Gate came into its own. You climbed up it on to the fence and jumped down into the garden next door to retrieve the ball - an exercise which took a long time, and sometimes proved in vain, for it was a large garden, with lots of undergrowth and growing vegetables, and there were many places where a ball could stay hidden forever. At any one time there must have been a dozen or so lying in that garden somewhere or other.

There was a feeling of excitement going over there, too, for it was forbidden territory, and you had to find the ball before old Mr Newham, who lived at the house at the bottom of the garden, came along; though truth to tell he was a kindly old boy, a retired farmer, who always threw the ball back promptly himself if it was in the garden at the time.

Many supposed fallen wickets were disputed in the shadow of the Side Gate: did the ball hit the chalk wicket? Did the bat hit it

A Childhood Like Ours...

in backswing? Was the crease reached with the bat - made by cutting two bits out of a short thin plank to leave a handle and flat blade - before the ball hit the wicket in an attempted run out?

The Side Gate stayed aloof and silent as the arguments went on, nor did it flinch if the bat was flung at it as the ousted batsman stormed off sulkily, to take his turn as the bowler (it was always much more fun to bat!).

Then there was tennis. The Side Gate made a fine practice wall, because of the unpredictability of its returns, though the passage was not wide enough to play tennis shots correctly. If the ball hit the wide horizontal cross support of the gate, or the diagonal support, which both strengthened the vertical planks in the structure; or indeed either of the large hinges at top and bottom which each reached a third of the way across the gate - if any of these bits were struck, the ball would shoot off in any direction or at any angle - a good test for reflexes.

Sometimes it would shoot off into Mr Newham's garden of course, and then the side gate became a climbing frame again...

It was a formidable tennis opponent, as the ball always came back in one way or another, unless you hit it over, and then it was out of play anyway. It was a dependable old object.

The Side Gate also featured in other sports - it was the turning point of races up and down the garden (you had to touch it as you turned), and when bowling an old pram wheel with a stick up and down the garden, you could rebound it off the gate to make your turn when you got expert at it. Something that took up hours of my time was seeing how many runs up and down the garden I could make before the wheel went out of control and fell.

Marbles was another game played by the Side Gate. There was an area of earth about six feet long between the gate and where

A Childhood Like Ours...

the concrete surface of the passage began, and we used to hollow out a little hole in it to play the marble game we called "bibby". Yet more time I would spend just throwing a ball against the gate and catching it, sometimes juggling it with two - a simple pastime, and again the gate did not make it easy for me with the angles at which it returned the ball.

It was certainly used to being climbed on, too, and not only for the reasons I have already mentioned. Just over the fence in Mr Newham's garden, close to the Side Gate, was an old greengage tree. It never bore much fruit, and had only one main branch in addition to the trunk, but it was easy to climb on to via the gate, and if a greengage was within reach we had it - usually before it was anywhere near ripe, of course, and it would usually give us a terrible stomach ache. Mr Newham never missed them, though, as there were never enough to make a crop to pick.

I and my brothers and sisters used to play games on that tree, too. When we were still in single figures as far as age was concerned it was The Faraway Tree of Enid Blyton's tales, and we were variously Saucepanman, Moon Face, Silky the Fairy, and so on; or we'd go up there and eat our elevenses in the school holidays.

There were apple trees nearby as well - on Mr Newham's side - which were always well laden with fruit. They always looked very tempting, and usually the temptation to climb the Side Gate and pick one overcame us. They were sour cookers, and had the same effect on us as the greengages, but they were not missed from the tree.

Other memories of the Side Gate are hazy, others still are fleeting but clear. I don't remember the first time I went beyond it as a child, but no doubt there was a time. I do recall, though, one occasion when I was perhaps three years old, our faithful wire-haired terrier, Binkie, leaping on to the top and scrambling

A Childhood Like Ours...

over. The gate was only five feet high, but when you are only two foot yourself it seems a formidable obstacle, and those few seconds stick in my memory as an awesome and wondrous sight.

Binkie was an obedient dog; another mongrel terrier we had, much later, called Tammy, was not, and he was ill-tempered too. If he were to get out in the garden on his own, the cry would go out as soon as he was missed indoors: "Is the Side gate closed? Close the side gate, quickly, before Tammy gets out on the road!"

For Tammy was inclined to take a nip at passers-by if he took a fancy to it!

I must have been about three when for a while I was afraid of the dustman. In those days they used to bring their own metal bins in, empty your dustbin into it, and take it back to the cart - there was none of this business of the householder having to take his bin to the roadside, and wheelie bins had certainly not been thought of.

Anyway, perhaps it was the sight of the dustman's head, in its cloth cap, and bin on shoulder, appearing over the Side Gate when I was playing one day in the passage; perhaps I was engrossed in the play and he startled me. But as he came up to me through the Side gate I remember him saying - no doubt in a quite friendly manner: "I'll teark yew away in my cart!"

Cheerily meant or not, it terrified me, and I went screaming to the back door, and an anxious Mum came out and picked me up. I remember being held in her arms and her chatting to Mr Knights (for that was the dustman's name) outside, and him again saying: "I'll teark yew away in moi cart!" It was a long time before I would go out in the passage on my own if I knew the dustcart was due, after that! In fact the dustman was probably among the brigade of tradesmen whose appearance

66

A Childhood Like Ours…

through the Side Gate was welcomed by we children - others were the baker, the milkman (I'd get a ride on his pony drawn cart, if I was lucky), the greengrocer, the sweep, the coalman, the insurance man - or dad coming home from work on his bike, an appearance especially welcome if it was Friday. That was payday at the printing works, and therefore "sweet night," when he brought us home a treat.

In the other direction the Side Gate was the exit to the outside world at various notable points in the lives of we children. For my own part, my first trip out in the pram I don't remember, but setting off for my first day at school, aged five, proud in my brown and yellow blazer and blue overcoat (they didn't match) I do; my first day going to grammar school, first trip to Norwich (to see the City play), my first trip to play football for the school, my first trip to catch the bus to Norwich to start my working life; and many others.

The Side Gate in its silent way bade me good luck on each occasion. Many's the time, too, that opening the Side Gate has brought a welcome end to a tiring day, a disappointing day, or a cold day.

Many are the friends, and relatives, and businessmen, with good and bad news, that came and went through that same Side Gate, which was often dilapidated and repaired, scratched and worn, damaged by wind when the lock was ill-fitting, when its banging in the wind kept you awake at night till it was mended next time…

I remember, after the handle with which you lifted the latch was finally lost forever, there was a round hole through which you put your finger to lift it manually; and there were times when, in its later years, you had to lift the gate itself and shove it heftily as you did so, to get it open - a difficult manouvre when you

A Childhood Like Ours...

were trying to get your bike and a heavy shopping bag in too, in gusty wind or rain, having done the weekly errands for Mum after school. Many are the fingers it jammed in such circumstances over the years.

Those were the times when it didn't seem a friend, but there were many times when it did. In the winter, coming home from school in blustery wind and rain and snow, it brought you protection from the elements as soon as you were inside and had it closed (it faced east). I can remember when snow drifted up against it from the inside two or three feet deep - snow which had to be dug away before the Side Gate could be opened.

Snow lodged on the ledges of its cross supports and on top of the gate itself, where in the summer blue-tits, sparrows and robins, the occasional wren and many greedy starlings would sit and wait for crumbs that mum would scatter in the garden from the table cloth.

It may have looked dour, and grey and clumsy in its later years when it had been repaired with ill-matching pieces of wood, but the Side Gate had its own singular personality and atmosphere, and influenced the atmosphere of the passage, too. Its familiarity and participation in the comings and goings of the children of the house particularly made it a sentinel of security, gave it an unconscious homely warmth and friendliness.

The Side Gate was home and the garden and toast for tea and bedtime stories just as much as the tea-table and fireside chair and cosy bedclothes are part of those things.

Will that new wrought iron gate ever come to be known as the Side Gate to someone in years hence, and be looked upon with the same affection? May be it will. But its physical make-up will prevent it being used for the games we used it for, and the trees and garden next door were cleared and built on some time ago. The new gate has made the passage much lighter, but has taken

A Childhood Like Ours…

away the intimacy from it.
The Side Gate that our family knew and grew up with has gone forever, to rest eternally where all good gates may find repose. I never thought the time would come when an old wooden gate would bring a sentimental lump to the throat and a tear to the eye.
But now it has. Rest well, old friend.

A Childhood Like Ours…

The Black Dogs

YES, football - that was not only a game of the 1950s, of course, it is a game for every decade and every era since it was invented, and who did not kick a ball about from an early age, whatever type of ball it may be: tennis ball, bouncy rubber ball, proper football, even if it had a puncture? Stones in the road and tins cans sometimes had to suffice - we would kick anything and pretend it was a football and were scoring a magnificent goal.

I've mentioned our games in the passage. Whether that led to me supporting Bungay Town, The Black Dogs, from an early age, or whether the interest came first from Dad taking me to a game on The Rec (Earsham Recreation Ground, just over the bridge to Earsham on the right) I don't know. It was probably the latter, for Dad was an avid supporter and had been on the committee in the 1930s.

So I joined the Saturday afternoon pilgrimage to the Rec from an early age, probably four or five, when it was still the late 1940s, and the Black Dogs were in their heyday, winning the Norfolk and Suffolk League championship three years in a row, and the league cup. And they had some mighty games in the FA Amateur Cup too, then and in the early 1950s - Wycombe Wanderers, Hendon and Brentwood and Warley were among the teams to come to Bungay, and they never had an easy game against the fighting Black Dogs. I remember, when they played Hendon, seeing 13 coaches which had brought supporters from London, lined up on the Drift in Outney Road, which looked down over the Waveney water meadows.

Earsham Rec was part of those meadows, and would flood

regularly - not a season went by when games were not called off because of flooding, and I remember being at one game when you could see the water from the adjoining Waveney gradually creeping closer and closer to, and then on, the pitch, and the game having to be abandoned. The touch-line was no more than 10 yards from the river at its closest, and the ball would frequently land in the water, and someone - usually the Bungay trainer Ted Myall - would get his feet wet going in to retrieve it. In those days clubs could not afford to have any number of balls available so another could be used immediately, and it was a matter of waiting for the leather match ball to come back, sodden with water and even heavier than usual, so play could resume.

Referees came in for criticism, as they do today, and at Bungay the regular cry, when the crowd felt a bad decision had been made against them, was "Chuck the ref. in the river!"

But that never happened, as far as I know - the criticism and cat-calling was far more good-natured in those days than it is today.

Large crowds would follow the Black Dogs in those days - over 1000 was not unusual, and an average gate was 500-600 when they were doing well. Mum always reckoned she could hear the roar of the crowd from home in Southend Road, over a mile away.

I would make my way there with Dad, with the crowds getting larger as you approached the bridge and then turned onto the grassy drive which was the approach to the turnstile - just one - where Reggie Crisp, Billy King or some other committee member would take the money, 3d or 6d probably, and give you a ticket, and someone else would sell you a programme for 2d.

More often that not the crowd would be at least one deep all the way round the pitch, standing on the duckboards put there to prevent you standing on the always wet ground. Often I didn't get a good view, but I could see the ball when it was in the air, as it was a lot - it would fly higher than the tops of the trees that stood beside the river, and someone would inevitably shout: "That's the highest today!"

But I remember, in the early 1950s, when I was older and went on my own with brother Robin and met other boys there, we would often lay on our stomachs on the green grass behind the goal at the Earsham Dam end, and watch the goals go in. Bungay were prolific scorers in those days, and there was one chap who always stood behind the goal and would shout loudly every time the ball hit the net: "Hello! Wheel'em in, Bungay!"

That cry provided me with an apt title for my book on the history of the club 35 years later.

We got such joy and excitement out of going to watch the Black Dogs play in those days - many youngsters were among the crowd on the Rec., where an old nissen hut served as the primitive changing rooms and there was a tea hut beside it. The whole atmosphere of the crowds, and the chatter, and the cheers and groans, and the scent of the grass and the river running by, was unforgettable.

And at the end of the game, at around 4.45pm, as dusk gathered, we would run all the way home, either through the town or round the back of the hills, each wanting to tell Mum and Dad the score:

"Bags I tell them!"

"No, I'll tell them - you told them last time!"

"No I didn't!"

When we got there we would burst in through the back door and into the kitchen, and yell, breathlessly and simultaneously: "Bungay won 4-0!"

It was around 5pm. Mum always baked on Saturday afternoons and the aroma of hot chocolate buns baking in the gas oven

A Childhood Like Ours...

wafted through the adjoining living room where the wireless, on a small corner table by the window, was on. The familiar signature tune of Sports Report would be ringing out, or if it was a couple of minutes later when we arrived, the reading of the results would be well advanced. For some reason it was the names of the Scottish teams that remain embedded in my memory of those times - they seemed quaint somehow: Motherwell, East Fife, Stenhousemuir, Heart of Midlothian (always read in full then), Hamilton Academicals...
We were always keen to hear how Norwich and Ipswich had done, and Dad was a supporter of what he always referred to as The Arsenal.
They were warm memories. When Bungay moved to the Maltings Meadow as their headquarters in 1953, the atmosphere was never quite the same, and the crowds never as big, except for the big games against the likes of Kingstonian, Ilford, Harwich and Leytonstone. From that time I began to keep records of every game, and during one season I recorded the attendances too - by going round the pitch counting people. In the mid-fifties it was usually between 200-250 for ordinary league games.
I played for Bungay Minors, and then Bungay A from about 1957. We never did particularly well, and often lost heavily - I remember a 13-2 defeat on one occasion.
My most poignant memory of playing came in February, 1958, on the Saturday after the Munich air crash claimed the lives of eight of Manchester United's Busby Babes as well as others. We played Thorpe Minors that afternoon and we played on the first team pitch, something we did not often have the privilege of doing.
Before the game both teams lined up on the centre circle to observe two minutes silence in memory of those who died in

A Childhood Like Ours...

that tragedy, and even as I teenager I recall how emotional I felt. I looked at the green grass of the pitch, at the goals, and the hedgerows and blue sky - thousands of miles from Munich, hundreds from Manchester, Bungay Minors were a tiny dot in the football scene. Yet here we stood, united in national and international grief for young players who had the football world before them, and remembering and grieving. That scene was being repeated at hundreds of insignificant games at hundreds of venues around the country - a mark of the immense impact and shock that tragedy had on the wider footballing and sporting world.

As I write this, the 50th anniversary of that awful occasion has just been commemorated.

During the 1950s the Maltings Meadow was often the place we would kick a ball around, using jut one goal, and maybe only four or five of us playing. I had friends on Ditchingham Dam at the time - Graham and Ivan Button, Bobby Myall, Roger Harvey - and we would spend hours in the school holidays playing there, and getting worn out and thirsty. We played cricket too, and sometimes we would hire the tennis courts and play tennis, using Mum's old rackets, and threadbare balls.

We were never bored. There always seemed to be things to do. With others on the Dam - John and Margaret Harris, Maureen Smith (whose parents ran the garage there) and Maureen Flatt, we formed a club called The Chicken Club (not sure why the name was chosen, there were no chickens on the roundabout then - indeed there was no bypass roundabout!) and each of us had a code name. John edited a magazine to which we all contributed. It lasted only a few weeks, as such things did in those days, till you moved on to some other idea. But it was by the river on Ditchingham Dam that we played boat races with sticks on the water, or a game we invented called Snakes, which

A Childhood Like Ours…

involved jumping across a shallow dry dyke there – a sort of tag. It was on Ditchingham Dam that we would sometimes, in the holidays, sit and collect car numbers, jotting them down as cars went by. The fact that we could wait some time between cars was an indication of how quiet the roads were (the Dam was the main road to and from Bungay and Norwich of course) in the 1950s, but we still got a pretty good list in the course of a day. Numbers beginning with EX were a popular series to collect because they indicted local cars and so there were plenty of them. Three letter indexes ending in BJ, PW and CL also indicated they were sold by local car dealers and there would be plenty of them going to and fro.

We went for bike rides. The Buttons' father, Walter Button, was a photographer, and sometimes we would bike to Loddon to take completed photographic orders to the chemists there, and bring back to him undeveloped films for processing.

They were good days, growing up days, healthy outdoor days, and we never got into trouble - there was no time to. There was always something else to do.

I've digressed a bit from football, which was probably my greatest childhood love, and from the Black Dogs, who still play at the Maltings Meadow, with much-improved facilities, but with few regular supporters and the days of great exploits on the field now seeming a world away. The local game has changed so much in so many ways, and sportsmanship too often seems to take second place to winning.

But, on that same Maltings Meadow pitch, on that same Saturday as 50 years ago, today's players once again observed silence in memory of one of the world's great teams of an age ago, when sportsmanship and fairness were taken for granted….

A Childhood Like Ours...

Shopping and Deliveries

THE Tesco delivery van whizzes round towns and villages these days, taking the groceries to those who have ordered their weekly or monthly shop "on line." No need to actually talk to anyone, or be tempted by those extras you see on the shelves; no opportunity to pass the time of day with others out shopping.
No need to be sociable…
I suppose the Tesco van is the modern throw back to those days, the 1950s and before, when the pace of life was slower, mums and housewives were invariably at home, and individual tradesmen called at your door on a regular basis - the milkman, the baker, the paraffin man, the Man from the Pru, the grocer, and "mac" man, and so on.
As children the appearance of those tradesmen on the doorstep was eagerly looked forward too. I can just remember the time, it may not have been later than 1950, when Hancy's delivered the milk by pony and trap, and it was ladled out from a churn into a large jug - still warm from the cow sometimes, and certainly unpasteurised. I vividly remember the gentle sound of swirling milk as the metal pint-measure ladle, with its long handle to reach down into the churn, was dipped and then withdrawn and poured into the waiting jug. Memory tells me that this happened outside, beside the trap - obviously the churn was too heavy to carry to the door to do the ladling there, but I'm not sure what happened in wet weather - presumably the milk came indoors somewhat watered down!
It must have been around the early 1950s when bottles finally replaced that rural way of delivering milk - pint and half pint

A Childhood Like Ours…

bottles, with cardboard tops with a sketch of a cow on it.
But the real delight of the milk delivery was that sometimes Mr Hancy let you ride on the trap down to his next stop. It may only have been 20 yards down the road, but didn't we feel grand, standing there clutching the edge of the swaying trap, and hoping everyone in the road would see us!
The milkman came every day. The baker, Mr Eastaugh, came three days a week – Tuesdays, Thursdays and Saturdays, rapping on the back door and being welcomed in with his wicker basket piled high with a variety of loaves, crusty and still warm from the oven - the more burnt the crust the better as far as I was concerned. And sometimes he would have delicious cakes in his basket, and we would persuade mum to have some, though for us they were a luxury she could probably not afford. Cream doughnuts, jam doughnuts and cream horns were the favourites, but they could only be an occasional treat.
The loaves we had were usually either ordinary bloomers, or cottages loaves - we called them "nobble" loaves, because each of them had four crusty nobbles on them, which Mum would slice off for us and put butter on the inside - they were absolutely delicious. With the bloomers we would "bag" the top crust - that nice brown top of the loaf which again was eaten with a generous dollop of butter. The taste was heavenly - I can still conjure it up.
We loved the crusty part of the loaves - if you didn't get the top crust you wanted the side crust as the next best thing. Of course it meant the rest of the loaf was almost crustless and difficult to slice with the bread knife, and Mum and Dad were left mainly with the doughy centre. We children of the 1950s were probably indulged more than we should have been.
Both baker and milkman made a note of what was bought during the week, and on Saturdays they came with their leather

A Childhood Like Ours...

moneybag around their shoulders to collect payment. It was full of coins - halfpennies, pennies, threepenny bits, sixpences, shillings, half-crowns and maybe a few farthings, which were legal tender right through to 1960 - and I used to be absolutely fascinated to see them dip their hand in, making a money-jingling noise of copper and silver rubbing together, and bring it out with a huge handful of change to sort out the coins needed when offered a 10s note or £1 note in payment.

Of course we used to play at being milkman or baker in the garden, and the only way we could replicate that was with a bag of small stones picked from the flower beds. Those were the childhood days when, if asked what you wanted to be when you grew up, you would instantly say a milkman, or baker, or dustman, or lorry driver - a far cry from today's children who dream of being pop stars, or footballers, or dancers.

"Gilly" King was the greengroceries delivery man who always seemed to come on Saturdays when we were having dinner. He would knock on the door and march through into the dining-room, and Mum would get up and go out to his open-sided van to select what she wanted.

Again I would hang around, hoping to get a lift down to the next stop, and then sitting proudly in the passenger seat, enjoying the sensation, and seeing the long gearstick with its round black ball at the top vibrating as the vehicle moved off. We didn't have a car, so that ride was quite an adventure.

The paraffin man was Mr Whiteland, who usually came late on a Saturday afternoon, and Dad would go out for 3d worth of paraffin which he got in an old orange squash bottle. It was served through a small tap at the bottom of a large can, and smelt wonderful - as did the whole van, packed as it was with soaps, ands scourers, and sticks (for the fire), tins of Brasso and other polishes, and many other cleaning and hardware items.

A Childhood Like Ours…

The paraffin was not for a lamp as far as we were concerned - Dad got it mainly to help get the bonfire going if it was a trouble starting after he had been gardening, something which was a hobby he enjoyed more and more as the years went by, and after he had given up going to the football matches.
I can't remember which day the Man from the Pru (Mr Gladwell) came, and though he was a very friendly chap his visit was not so exciting, because it was simply a matter of Mum paying him the weekly or monthly amount for insurance, and he scribbling in her record book. So it was with the "mac" man, whose name I don't remember. We called him the "mac" man because mum bought our mackintoshes for school and paid by weekly instalments - which he came to collect for whichever company he represented.
An annual visitor to Southend Road was the scissor grinder. He would call to see if people needed any scissors, or shears or knives sharpening, and we would hang on the front gate and watch him at work, fascinated at the sparks flying from the grindstone on his barrow. It was equipped with a seat on which he sat, working the grindstone with a foot treadle, honing the item back to full sharpness.
I think he was a Romany gipsy, a big man, with a round, olive face made dirty by his work, and he always wore a trilby, and a collarless shirt, as he worked. He didn't say much, but I think he enjoyed us watching him, and he seemed to be surrounded by an aura of peace, and slight mystery in his pale blue eyes.
So there was a succession of callers at the house for us to look forward to and Mum to have a chat with and find out what the gossip was in the town. Other news Dad brought home from the printing works - always a hive of rumour and interesting chatter.
But the main grocery shopping was done at the Co-op in the town or the Flixton Road Stores which, as I have mentioned

A Childhood Like Ours…

elsewhere, we always called Bridges because it was run by Cyril and Beryl Bridges. One of we children, often me, would walk down there after school with the shopping bag and list of items to get, collecting the family allowance (7s 6d a week in the early 1950s if I remember rightly) while we were there, to pay for them. It was quite a small shop, with the sub-post office to the right as you went in, groceries to the front, and the sweet and ice-cream counter over to the left - it was there that we often spent our Saturday pocket money.

Getting the errands from the Co-op was usually a Thursday job, also after school, and I went on my bike. There, we put them "on the book," and would pay for them on Saturday after Dad had brought home the weekly wage on Friday night. Each item was asked for individually - there was no self-service - from several assistants working behind the counters, with each in their own section - cooked meat, cheese, sugar and flour, and so on. In those days a grocery shop was that - it sold groceries and left others to sell fruit and vegetables, or hardware. That was why in the 1950s there were several greengrocers shops in Bungay, several grocers and several hardware shops.

It was a true co-operative - CWS, the Co-operative Wholesale Society, and everyone had a share number - I remember ours as if it was yesterday because I gave it out hundreds of times when paying for items. It was 3393, and the dividend it paid, I think just before Christmas (though it may have been half-yearly or quarterly) was invaluable in helping to make ends meet.

That dividend was one of three "bonuses" Mum and Dad could reasonably confidently budget for when juggling the household outgoings. Another was Dad's annual bonus from the printing works, or Charter Money as it was always called. That was usually a very useful amount, and no doubt went some way towards paying the fees to send us to St Mary's School.

A Childhood Like Ours…

The third was the gas meter bonus. The meter man came to empty it every so often - probably every quarter - unlocking the money box and pouring out the coppers (1d pieces) and shillings (12d) that the meter took. It was an ancient system in which you put the coin in a slot and then turned a knob to make it drop to operate the gas system. The meter was in a rather awkward position, in a cupboard under the draining board beside the sink. One penny kept the supply going for some time, but you had to be sure you had some pennies and shillings handy to top it up. It was easier for children to put the money in, and we loved doing it, and seeing the flame on the gas ring surge again. The gas works which served the town was in Rose Lane which, appropriately, ways called Gas House Lane in those days.

Anyway, once the meter man had counted out the coins, he did his calculations in his accounts book with his pencil and gave Mum her rebate. I don't know how much money was in the meter each time, or what the rebate percentage was, but Mum always seemed pleased - though that was probably because it ensured meals on the table.

That may sound dramatic, but it was the way of life for many Bungay families, and no doubt families up and down the country. In those days, less than 10 years after the end of the second world war, there was little if any spare cash after the household bills were paid, and any extra that came along was like manna from heaven.

Times were hard - but by and large, families were secure units, and happy, and children were greatly cared for.

A Childhood Like Ours…

The Shed

AS children it was our early years Everest. Could we really scale its summit?
The footholds and handholds were not generous, and in early attempts I had to be content with staying on the first foothill, the lower cross plank of the door, and look up wistfully, and a little nervously, to the top. It seemed so high and out of reach to us children.
But Robin had made it, and so would I in time, with courage. And I did, finally being bold enough after weeks and months of attempts - and after growing a few more vital inches - to get a hand-hold on the roof itself, with the door open almost flat against the side.
A final heave, breathless with nervous emotion, a mixture of fear, and triumph, and not wanting to be seen to lack courage, and I was beyond the top cross plank, with one knee on the roof. A helping hand from Robin, the other leg stretched up and over, flat on to the roof, and I was there!
Joy and immense elation! I was on the shed roof for the first time, and the ground seemed far below as I lay and peeped over the edge (in truth it was about eight feet) and the blue, blue summer sky (it was always blue, wasn't it?) that little bit nearer.
At first I just crouched there, almost rigid, not daring to move. But as I acclimatised I gingerly stood up, and took steps across the shallow-pitched roof. I spotted mum at the sink in the kitchen 20 yards away, and waved frantically and proudly to attract her attention. And when she saw me her heart no doubt went into her mouth, but she waved back, just the same.
Soon I moved more confidently, and began to take in the views -

A Childhood Like Ours…

mainly the next-door-neighbours' gardens - with Mr Thornton's stagnant pond, and Mr Newham's summer house. Further away down the end of Southend Road was the Tower Mill, which had lost its sails many years ago, and was now a private house, occupied by a strange, stern-looking lady who kept a lot of cats.
Beyond that were the woodyard fields, with logs of willows laid out for seasoning by Edgar Watts, the company that made willow clefts for cricket bats which were used by many of the greatest Test cricketers around the world. The company's sawmills were at the other end of Southend Road, and sometime we would go down there with Dad, with a barrow, and get off-cuts for the fire.
And beyond that field were the beautiful St Mary's Fields, before they built houses on them. In early summer they were red with poppies, a stunning sight also viewed from Mum and Dad's bedroom window.
To the north was the town, and the tower of St Mary's Church, strong and dominant against the blue sky; and to the west the grazing meadows and fens, and the pencil tower of Earsham Church.
Right against the shed was a silver birch tree. Ah yes, THE silver birch tree, for was ever a single tree so beautiful to us, and so homely? It stood just on the neighbour's side of the bordering privet hedge, but Mum and Dad had watched it grow in the years they had been at 32, Southend Road, and cherished it as their own. It still stands there today as an enduring sentinel of our childhood garden.
As I stood on the shed roof for the first time, all those summers ago, the fresh green leaves and catkins of that tree brushed my face, and the aroma from them, warmed as they were by the sun, filled the air.
There is much that is idyllic about Bungay, but I can think of

A Childhood Like Ours…

nothing more so than lying on my back on the warm shed roof and looking up at the blue sky through the green leaves and catkins of the silver birch tree. Was any sight ever more naturally beautiful, ever more evocative of a happy childhood, with the sweet scent of the adjoining privet hedge, hard against the shed, wafting up to us? I can think of none.

These mingled and blended with the smell of the tar-pitch roof also heated, to a considerable degree, by the sun beating down on it. A strong scent, but a pleasant one, and symbolic now of memorable, lazy, hazy school summer holidays. So often, after that initial scaling of the shed, would I lay on that hot shed roof, beneath the sun and the gently waving birch tree, and sunbathe and read for hours, the favourite books of the day: The Famous Five, the Secret Seven, Just William, Billy Bunter, Biggles, or something a bit different, The Policeman's Holiday.

Every day was sunny, it seemed, and I only climbed down for lunch, though in truth we found many other things to do in the school holidays.

Getting down from the shed roof was easy, and getting up was easier the second time, as with most things. When I became a seasoned shed roof squatter I even dared to jump from it to the ground, onto a nearby patch of grass beside the apple trees, to show daring and strength, and hoped everyone was watching.

I even got my little sister, Jasmine, up on to the roof, though as she was the youngest she was more frightened than us boys, and never really enjoyed it, I think.

The shed was a great focal point of our young lives in the 1950s, because it had always been there, with its black pitch roof, fading green paint, single window and ill-fitting door, and filled with Dad's carpentry tools, workbench, gardening tools, our bikes and a considerable amount of rubbish, not to mention the big black spiders' webs among the wooden ceiling joists.

A Childhood Like Ours…

It had been built close up to the boundary fence, leaving a narrow gap into which I could just squeeze, and where unwanted rubbish was deposited - bits of wood, old bike parts and so on. And at the back of the shed there was just enough room to put a hutch for Robin's white mice. Where could they have gone if it had not been for the shed?

Those areas at the back and side were good places for hide-and-seek and other games. The shed itself was our log cabin when we made fires just outside, with matches - smuggled from the kitchen (where they lay ready to light the copper fire for Wednesday night baths) and boiled water on it in an old saucepan. To get the water to actually boil was another childhood triumph.

And then there were the drama productions. Had Drury Lane ever seen anything like them? Somehow we built a precarious stage in front of the shed door, and attached to the shed, from old planks and

A play on the makeshift stage in front of the shed in 1951! As with many cameras in those days, it let a lot of light in!.

other bits of wood nailed together with nails found in one of Dad's shed drawers, and even rigged up a sort of curtain. How it stayed up we never knew, but it did, and the shed served as the changing room for the productions, in which there were always three characters - villain, hero and damsel. Remaining brother and sister were younger and probably made up the audience with Mum and Dad, seated on the dining room chairs we brought out, and charged a halfpenny or penny for the privilege.

The plays did not last very long, with minimum script, but the costumes were from the dressing up bag and all the drama was crammed into a few minutes of stage action that was, of course, always warmly applauded by the small but appreciative audience!

Memories of childhood are often stimulated by aromas. The inside of the shed had those too - sawdust and shavings on the floor and oil on the bikes which were kept there out of the rain, along with the part used tins of paint on the shelves and the turpentine ("turps") used to clean the brushes.

The decor of the shed was highly colourful because its walls were used to clean the brushes on more often than not, after painting stints indoors, or in the shed. It was there that Dad, a gentle man in every sense of the word, made wooden toys for his children for Christmas - soldiers, farm animals, building bricks, and the marvellous one of a man walking down a slope on his own, unaided by clockwork or any other device except his own impetus - and where we tried out our own carpentry skills when we got the chance, using his tools. We ran indoors, crying for plasters on fingers and thumbs banged with ill-aimed hammers on many occasions over the years.

Chisels, planes, bradawls, saws, screwdrivers and hammers all had a fascination for us, and many were the cuts and blisters we got from misusing them, and the gardening tools stored there.

A Childhood Like Ours…

Sometimes we would try to dig down to Australia (because people said it was directly on the opposite side of the world) in the area just outside the shed, and we would sit at the shed entrance and have our elevenses that Mum brought out for us - usually a cup of cocoa and a digestive biscuit, or orange squash in the summer, and always exactly at 11am. We never achieved our goal of course, but we usually dug down to pure sand (about three feet at the most) and gleefully brought out buckets of it to play with on the concrete area under the kitchen window, where the sun warmed that hard surface, and the water we got from the rain butt had its own refreshing smell.

The shed was a ship, or a log cabin, or a cave, or a ranch or a wild west saloon, according to the games we played. And we were always slightly fearful about what was under it - it was slightly raised from the ground, so there was room under it into which we would sometimes peer, lying on our stomachs.

More cobwebs there, of course, and were there rats? Maybe. Childish minds imagined seeing many spookie things there.

That beautiful, idyllic birch tree is still there today, and so is the privet hedge. But the shed has long since gone and has been replaced by a summer house. It is a pleasant enough building, but it is too neat and clean to have the romance, mystery and allure that the old shed conjured up.

They were happy garden days of the 1950s, rich in activities. Do I envy all those things modern children have available to them but still say they are bored?

Not one bit…

A Childhood Like Ours…

Indoors

THERE probably were times when I was bored as a 1950s child, but of course you don't remember them - you only remember the many things you did do.
The truth is there were always things to do when there was "nothing to do" - those times you filled by reading or writing, and writing was with a fountain pen and an exercise book, not on a computer. I used to write childish fiction, adventure stories, with great apologies to Enid Blyton!
Those times when there was nothing to do were mainly when we were confined to indoors during the holidays by the weather. The last resort at times like that was to tidy out the toybox, which Dad had made from an old orange box. It sat beside the wireless, and indeed we used it to sit on when listening to the wireless - you had to sit close to it to hear it, because there always seemed to be lots of atmopsherics and high-pitched sounds coming from it even if you did seem to have the needle exactly on the right wavelength for the Light Programme, or Home Service, the two main ones we listened to in those days. As small children we listened to Toy Town, Children's Hour, Listen with Mother, and so on. Later, as we got older, it was Dick Barton - Special Agent, or Adventure Unlimited, or Journey Into Space. And as we became interested in pop music, we could, with difficulty, get Radio Luxembourg, on which they played the top 20, from 20 to 1, at 11pm on a Sunday night.
Other programmes were Lenny the Lion, or Round the Horn on Saturday lunch-times or, as I have mentioned elsewhere, Sports Report at 5pm on Saturday. Mum, of course, liked Mrs Dale's Diary, and in the evening I remember her enjoying Book at

A Childhood Like Ours…

Bedtime. She usually sewed, or darned socks while listening.
But that toy box was the seat you sat on to listen - if you could shut it, because lots of things were put in there in a hurry when clearing up, and eventually the lid would not shut properly and so, on a day when there was nothing else to do, you tidied it out.
Dinky cars and lorries, building bricks, bits of plasticine, soldiers, balls, skittles, dolls, crayons, pencils, broken bits of toys, toy baking things such as rolling pins, old Christmas cards, scraps of paper - there was everything in there, and we would empty them all out on to the floor.
Then it was a matter of deciding what could be thrown away and what should be kept - squabbles over that usually - in order to put everything back tidily so that the lid would fit properly again. By that time it would be nearly dinner time and we would be getting hungry, so the job might get left till later. I liked to put everything back meticulously tidily so I knew where to find it next time, but that did not always work.
That was being bored. In truth it did not happen often - there always seemed something or other to occupy me when it was wet or cold outside, and it usually happened on or around the dining-room table, which was always in the centre of the dining room, its sliding extension leaves at either end, in the "in" position until they needed to be drawn out for meals.
That was the table the family had meals at, three times a day, for all my childhood - a solid oak table, with stocky, spiral shaped legs, round which we sat in exactly the same position for each meal.
It was the first place parcels were put after shopping expeditions, before things were put away; we made Christmas trimmings on it on Christmas Eve, after going down to Bridges' to buy the coloured strips of paper to make into linking rings, using paste made from flour and water. We would sit at it to do

our school homework, or competitions for Uncle Jack's Corner (later the Cobbers Club) in the *Beccles and Bungay Journal,* as the cosy open fire burned nearby in the winter.

And the games we played on it! Pelmanism was a favourite on rainy holiday days in the 1950s - the 52 playing cards, laid out closely side by side, would fit exactly on the surface of the table with one leaf out. Another wet day favourite pastime was sorting out the cigarette cards, kept in a large box in the dining room cupboard (which also served as the airing cupboard). They had been collected by Mum and Dad in the 1930s and had fascinating images - some photographs, some sketches and some caricatures - of wrestlers, footballers, animals, birds, national flags, military decorations, historic buildings and many other subjects that kept us absorbed for hours, sorting them into order.

That table was our desk for painting pictures, or writing stories, letters, or Christmas cards at, or making all manner of things, from jumping beans made of silver paper and ball bearings from Mr Harmer's cycle repair shop to the cardboard models of houses or vehicles which you got from Weetabix packets; or Meccano constructions.

I played shove ha'penny with myself for hours on that table, with the lines of the timber joins around it proving ideal for the pitch perimeter markings; or Subbuteo table soccer. I made my own teams, with matchsticks and discarded trouser buttons for the base, painted team colours on them with my Rowney or Reeve's watercolour paints, and ran a little league with the teams.

Despite its limited dimensions that table also served as a table-tennis table, with a makseshift "net" made from wooden building bricks - in the 1950s, improvisation was the keynote when it came to finding things to do and games to play. The excitement and competition created within the confines of the

A Childhood Like Ours…

dining room provided some memorable matches between family and friends, and honed our skills for later exploits in the Bungay and District Table Tennis League in the Church Youth Club (home matches were at the Trinity Rooms) or Young Conservatives teams. It could easily have been Wembley arena.

And in the autumn it was on that table that we gleefully turned out our pockets full of conkers, collected from the trees in the Vicarage garden in Upper Olland Street (now Holmwood residential home for the elderly) and sorted out the biggest and best for stringing, and taking to school to play.

Mum kept the table well polished. Her routine was religious and every Friday afternoon was polishing time - red Cardinal polish for the stone kitchen floor, and Mansion polish for the furniture. Perhaps it is why that table has lasted so long, and still has a shine today.

It was also Mum's ironing board. She would lay an old blanket on the table, and would rest the electric iron (with its round plug) on an old flat Players cigarette tin to protect the table surface from the heat - improvisation again, when a proper ironing board was a luxury. Sitting on one side of the table, doing homework or writing stories, warmed by the heat of the iron and scent of newly ironed linen, and the open fire glowing nearby, is one of the cosiest of childhood memories.

That table played a part in our young lives in so many ways as it stood there, steadfastly, in the middle of the room, over the years. It was taken for granted, unnoticed almost - but what would we have done without it? Another of those inanimate objects which yet has a character all of its own.

A Childhood Like Ours...

The Trinity Rooms

CONCERTED efforts are being made in Bungay at the moment to find a site, and funding, to build a new community centre for the town - a one-stop shop which would provide a meeting and function hall the town can be proud of, and a home for other social and community services.

It will replace the old, outdated community centre in Upper Olland Street, which started life as a war time Army hut before being re-erected on part of the former Honeypot Meadow for use as a Ministry building at around the time the welfare state was founded.

Hopefully, the dedicated efforts will be successful and Bungay will have a modern building to use.

In the 1950s, the King's Head Hotel was the venue for many of the town's top civic and social events - the Town Dinner, Rotary Club meetings, weddings, dances, Christmas festivities, public meetings would take place there, or over the road at The Three Tuns Hotel, the other prominent venue with a fine ballroom and banquet hall. Both were historic coaching inns, well used by people visiting the town.

But as a child and teenager of the 1950s my main memories as far as going to events was concerned were of the Trinity Rooms. They stood in Wharton Street, where the library now is, and initially were built alongside the ancient Wharton almshouses, which were demolished at the end of the 1920s to make way for the then new fire station on the corner of Lower Olland Street, and later three council houses.

The Trinity Rooms - built in the 1890s as the church hall for Holy Trinity Church when it was a separate parish, alongside St

A Childhood Like Ours…

Mary's parish - were held in great affection by the general populace of Bungay because almost everyone, at some time or other, must have had reason to go there. They were in use every day of the week, including weekends, because that was where Sunday School was held, and of course the other church activities - parochial church council meetings, Mother's Union, Young Wives and so on. The Women's Institute met there, the church youth club met there, the Sunday School Christmas parties were held there, and as well as those things public meetings, private birthday parties, fundraising events such as jumble sales, bring and buy sales, bazaars, quizzes, beetle drives, celebration parties for such things as the Coronation - the list was endless.

The facilities were versatile. You entered from the street through the quite narrow double doors into an equally narrow foyer where coats and hats and umbrellas were hung, and just to the right was the entrance to the main hall, high ceilinged and with a stage at the far end. Down to the left another door led into another small room sometimes used for small meetings, and beyond that was another larger meeting room.

That room was connected to the air raid shelters, built at the start of the second world war and later used for storage purposes. Also off that first small room was the kitchen, with basic kitchen facilities, and through that you came to another small meeting room, and then the billiard and snooker room (which could also be reached through a door on the left of the entrance foyer).

Altogether it was something of a rabbit warren, but a venue where several meetings could be held at any one time. As well as the main door, there was also access down a narrow passage which divided the main rooms and the air raid shelter.

Sunday School was held at 3pm in the main hall, and was well attended in the 1950s when for many families it was still routine. It was taken by Miss Larner, beloved by generations of Bungay children as a teacher at Bungay Primary School, who would conduct proceedings from the stage, producing an aura of gentleness and peace and in complete command of the children in that way.

It's strange the things that stick in your mind. As a child at St Mary's School, when the register was called each morning we would answer, "Present," but at the primary school they answered, "Yes, Miss," and of course the primary school children did that at Sunday School too. Not many St Mary's children went to Sunday School in Bungay because a lot of them came from the villages around, so for me saying "Present" seemed a bit out of place among all the Yes, Misses. I remember feeling somewhat self-conscious about what to say when my name was called.

Occasionally the Vicar, the Rev (later Canon) William Lummis would take Sunday School. He was a military man (he became a leading authority on the Victoria Cross), and expected instant response to what he said. He found it difficult to cope with young children who were not immediately quiet, and I vividly recall one occasion when Wilfred Carr was playing him up, he called him out to the front, hit him across the face once, and told him to go home!

It seemed out of character, but having been through the grim realities of the second world war when obeying commands was vital, coping with a Sunday School class must have seemed completely different territory. He was a very religious man, with a kind heart, and I'm sure the incident hurt him, inwardly.

After the initial part of Sunday School - a hymn, story and prayers - Mr Lummis took the older boys through to the small inner room between the billiard room and the kitchen, to lead a discussion group on a topic from the Bible. There were never any problems there, but I recall little of the nature of the discussion.

It was Mr Lummis who would lead the courses for those preparing for confirmation, too, though they took place in the vestry at St Mary's Church - about five evening sessions of about half an hour each, as far as I can remember.

The church youth club at Trinity Rooms was always well attended, and there was no religious element to that. There was badminton in the main hall, table tennis in the other larger room, billiards of course (we didn't play snooker, it was only later that that took over in popularity from the three-ball game), and others would gather on stage to listen to music on the record player. The popular hits of the time were played over and over again, with Connie Francis, Alma Cogan and Elvis Presley the up and coming singers of the day.

Equipment for the various activities, as well as other Sunday School paraphernalia, was stored in the air raid shelter, into which there was direct access. The black-out curtains remained in place in the shelter until it was demolished in the early 1990s.

The Sunday School Christmas parties were always held there of course - from 4pm-6pm, with everyone sitting down to tea at trestle tables to start with, with sandwiches, cakes, jelly, ice-creams, and wearing party hats from the crackers. There were games, and the inevitable visit from Father Christmas to hand out gifts.

During elections, both national and local, the Trinity Rooms were always used as a polling station, with big banners outside the doors. And it was also at the Trinity Rooms that families went to collect their new ration books when the old ones ran out of points. Blood donor sessions were regularly held there, and I remember going there, from the grammar school, and lining up for tuberculosis screening jabs.

And on Saturdays it was the venue for fundraising events such as jumble sales - almost every organisation in the town had at least one jumble sale a year, it seemed - or general sales. Long queues would form up outside in advance of the opening time, to get the best bargains, and once inside there was hubbub as people jostled to the front to sort through the goods, pick something up and ask the price - usually 2d or 3d - and stuff it into their shopping bag.

Those rooms were versatile and well loved. They may not have been the warmest place in winter, and the roof may have leaked occasionally, but in the 1950s they were very much a focal point of Bungay life, and there was a lot of sadness and some controversy when the church decided to sell the premises, rather than meet the ever mounting maintenance costs and the cost of bringing them up to modern health and safety standards of the 1990s.

A Childhood Like Ours…

Music and Dancing

MP3 players, iPods, Walkmans – you can have music with you wherever you are. Even mobile phones play music these days! Today's youngsters would be aghast at how primitive access to the popular tunes of the day was back in the 1950s.

Indeed in the years immediately after the war, little had changed from pre-war days. Mum and Dad had a wind up gramophone, and a heavy playing arm which you put manually on to the record after winding up the machine, releasing the brake so the old 78rpm record would turn, and after checking that there was a needle in the head – they had to be changed frequently.

That was our first introduction to music, and the music we played was largely pre-war records which were parents' favourites, and which we also came to enjoy because there was nothing else. So we would put on the 12-inch records – Paul Robson singing such songs as Old Man River, and way Down upon the Swannee River, or The Old Rugged Cross. Or there would be a brass band – I can't remember which one – playing for the singing of The Boys of the Old Brigade, to which we would march round the dining-room table in step to the music.

But there was humour too – among the collection was the original Runaway Train, and the hilarious Laughing Policeman, not to mention non-musical records. I particularly remember the Mr and Mrs Brown series: Mr and Mrs Brown at Wembley, or The Races, or on other outings.

It was a His Master's Voice gramophone, with the little dog looking down the hole from whence the voice came, and is was some time before we cottoned on to the fact that there was NOT

A Childhood Like Ours...

a little man down there somewhere singing or talking. It was one of the mysteries of childhood!

It was on that gramophone that we played the first records we bought – Marion Ryan singing Mr Wonderful was my first, followed by my first 45rpm record, a revolution at the time. That was a compilation of six pop songs of the time, but not by the singer who got them into the charts.

The music industry really took off in the 1950s, of course. Down at the Maltings Meadow, the popular songs would blast out over the public address system before Bungay's matches started – Doris Day with the Deadwood Stage, Jimmy Young with Ever More, Alma Cogan (or was it Eve Boswell) with Pickin' a Chicken, and others by Dickie Valentine, or Ruby Murray.

In the mid-fifties Bill Haley and his Comets exploded on to the scene with Rock Around the Clock, and Tommy Steele and Elvis Presley became the heart-throbs either side of the Atlantic. Michael Holliday, Perry Como, David Whitfield, and then Buddy Holly, James Dean, and Frankie Vaughan, Connie Francis, Frank Ifield, Cliff Richard and The Shadows, Dean Martin and many others came tumbling into our homes via Radio Luxembourg, or the Juke Box at Alfo's Café in the Market Place, and sent us out to Booty's in Earsham Street to buy their records.

Eventually we got the luxury of an electric record player, on which you could pile 10 records at a time, and watch fascinated as each one in turn dropped on to the turntable on top of the other. It was a great decade for pop music.

But the mix was still there. As I mention in the chapter on the grammar school, we were introduced to classical music by having it played to us at assembly each morning; the dancing classes run at the secondary modern school in Hillside Road

A Childhood Like Ours…

East by Harry and Phyllis Blowers were popular on Friday evenings and we would learn the basic steps of the waltz, quickstep and foxtrot to the sound of Victor Sylvester's Band. Harry took the boys, lined up on one side of the hall, through the male steps and Phyllis took the girls, lined up on the other, through their steps. When it came to putting what we had learned into practice, there was a mad rush by the boys to grab the favourite girls, with the inevitable wallflowers being left to the last.

Many romances were begun – some eventually leading to marriage – at those Friday evening session as adolescents rutted and strutted!

There were regular dances around the Bungay area to put our efforts into practice, with a number of popular dance groups in being. The Delta Five was one I remember particularly, often booked for dances at the Chaucer Institute, or the King's Head Hotel ballroom, or the Three Tuns Hotel ballroom – the three main dance venues in the town. Those were the days when the boys always wore suits and Brylcreem and a tie to go out and the girls' full skirts and lots of hair lacquer.

Harry and Phyllis's dance classes were legendary, and we also learned the then modern jive, and the old fashioned dances, such as the barn dance, Valeta, Gay Gordons and the old fashioned waltz. But their days were numbered with the advent of the Twist and Locomotion and Jitterbug and other modern trends, as the memorable music of the fifties moved into the even more vibrant Swinging Sixties…

A Childhood Like Ours...

Biking and Walking

WHENEVER I walk up Outney Road to the Common - which is frequently - it brings back memories of the day I learnt to ride a bike.
For it was in Outney Road that I learnt. I was good friends with the Wortleys, who lived in Waveney Cottage on the Drift there - Sandy, Jonathan (who was my age) Sarah, and George - and Terry (Squiggy) Squire was also part of our group.
They could already ride their bikes, and they determined to teach me to ride. It was a summer's day, and Sandy got his bike up from the cottage's garden on to the road, with the others looking on and encouraging me. I sat on the bike, gripping the handlebars tightly and nervously, with Sandy holding it. He pushed and I steered (erratically) and we went off towards the common, Sandy still holding the seat and I beginning to pedal. At the iron gate that led on to the Little Common we stopped and I managed to stumble off, then re-mounted and we followed the same procedure all the way back. It felt OK, and we decided to do another run, from opposite the Webster Street junction, along the spontaneous cycling training course in front of the picturesque St Edmund's almshouses with their mock Tudor chimneys.
This time I didn't wobble so much, and it felt better, and the steering was straighter. When I got to the Common gate that time I managed to stop without falling over, and I turned round to Sandy.
He wasn't there - he was still standing adjacent to the almshouses waving, and the others started cheering. I had ridden a hundred yards on my own! I could ride a bike!

A Childhood Like Ours…

I turned the bike round, got on, and set off back, hands gripping the handlebars tightly, but staying up. Yes! I could ride a bike!
It was an exhilarating feeling, one of those steps in the progress of a young life completed, and I couldn't wait to get home to tell Mum and Dad. Next day I borrowed Sandy's bike and I and Jonathan and Sarah and Squiggy went for a ride down over Earsham Dam. We decided to turn into School Road and go down to the Mill. Turning a corner was another matter, a new discipline, but I managed it with trepidation and managed to stay up. But at the end of School Road, making the turn left to the Mill, I wasn't so successful - I came a cropper, to use a colloquial Suffolk phrase of the day. The road had been newly surfaced - we had watched it being done a few days previously. First the tarring lorry spreading the shiny, steaming strong smelling tar evenly over a stretch of 200 yards or so, then the lorry evenly tipping its load of granite chips on to the tar, and then the steam roller moving into position, smoke billowing from its tall chimney and its engine chugging away, to roll the chips into the tar and complete the bonding. Some chips and tar adhered to the huge front roller and the big rear wheels but it completed its job. Watching roads being surfaced with that method is a quintessential memory of the 1950s (and probably years before that) for many children.
Anyway, two or three days after that surfacing at Earsham I fell off the bike and my knee and hands came into firm contact with some of those granite chips and mingled tar, breaking the skin on both so that red blood quickly mingled with the black pitch. I winced and got up and brushed the loose chips from my wounded knees and hands and wiped the blood away with my handkerchief. Both would need Elastoplasts.
It was an early reminder that being able to fully control a bike would take a little longer. And an abiding memory of that tiny

moment of my life was the aroma of tar and granite which was close to my face for a moment when I fell. It was not an unpleasant smell, rarely sensed today but when it is it always reminds me immediately of that episode.

Of course virtually every child owned a bike in those days and mine duly arrived on my 10th birthday - a shining New Hudson model, and it got plenty of use. Going on bike rides was a regular pastime after that, though I well remember the first time I biked to Beccles, with Robin. We decided to take a picnic lunch and eat it on The Cut, which we did. But as soon as we had finished I felt terribly home sick, and pedalled back there and then to Bungay as fast as I could!

That feeling soon passed and I biked there regularly after that. One year I biked to Lowestoft every day for a week to take part in the Lowestoft Junior Tennis tournament, and on another occasion I recall meeting David Trafford one Easter Monday. He was going to bike to Minsmere, so I and Robin went with him. It was a very windy day and it was hard work, but we made it there and back. And one year, I think 1957, Robin and I went on a biking holiday, spending a week staying at youth hostels - our route took in overnight stops at Saffron Walden, Reading, Arundel, Hastings, Tunbridge Wells and Castle Hedingham, and home from there.

Biking was how people got about in the 1950s - that or walking. We enjoyed going for walks, on a Sunday usually, or on any day during the school holidays. Up Annis Hill to Mettingham and back was a favourite one, and another was Bath Hills Lane. Either with family members or with the Wortleys and the rest of the gang we would cross the Common, over the bridge over the old river and then over to Ditchingham via the narrow bridge over the Waveney which still bears the inscription, H N Rumsby, Town Reeve 1922, and then across the drive which

A Childhood Like Ours…

leads to Ditchingham Lodge, and up the slope to Bath Hills lane. You had to walk in single file. Half way along the path there is a dog-leg turn and there were always rumours in those days - perhaps it was just children's talk - that a ghost lurked there. Whether there were any mysterious origins for that rumour I don't know - but I do know that no one wanted to be last in line when we passed that spot, and it did seem that a strange, shivery sensation ran through you in that vicinity. We never dallied there. Uncanny, perhaps, or just the story playing on our imaginations.

Towards the end of the path was Target - Target Hill in the days around the turn of the 19th-20th century, when the 3rd Suffolk Rifles Company would set up their targets there for practice and fire at them from the other side of the river. The footpath was along the top of Bath Hills and the targets at the bottom, at river level. It was a very steep hill, and we always dared ourselves to scramble down to the bottom, and then up again. I'm not sure what the gradient was but it was probably greater than one-in-two, and if you started to slide on the loose earth on the way down it was difficult to stop. We had a few tumbles there.

At the top of the hill stood an old beech tree, on which numerous children carved their initials with the pen knives or sheath knives many carried, quite innocently, in the 1950s. If we had a picnic with us we would sit and eat it under that tree, or play among the trees which wooded Bath Hills. They still do - and carved initials can still be identified on the beech tree, though Target Hill is now fenced off as private land, and no longer can the new generation of youngsters enjoy the excitement and danger of clambering up and down it.

I mentioned knives. Yes, pretty well everyone aged between, say, eight and 15 had a knife, and of course it was a routine item for a Boy Scout to carry. There were single blade penknives with which your sharpened your pencils at school, carved initials, cut branches from hedgerow to make bows and arrows, or pop-guns, or for many other uses. Others had penknives which had a variety of things - they are called Swiss knives though we never referred to them as that. They had two blades, a corkscrew for opening bottles, an opener for getting the tops off bottles - Vimto was popular in the 1950s - and that long rounded blade with a point which was always referred to as "a thing for getting stones out of horses' hooves." Never having had a horse I never used it for that, but it was put to many other uses, and of course came in useful for a variety of fishing needs, or when stringing conkers.

Many boys had sheath knives, too. I was really proud of mine, with its shining blade topped by a handle formed from a goat's foot, or the foot of a small deer, with its fur still attached and a strong leather sheath. I remember that I got it from one of those jumble sales at the Trinity Rooms mentioned elsewhere in this book, and I was really proud of it, wearing it on the belt of my jeans most of the time when I was not at school.

It had the same use as a penknife, but was usually sharper, and certainly better for making pop-guns with lengths of elder wood from which you took out the pithy centre and then made a handle to fit down it. An acorn or something similar was pressed tightly into one end for the missile, and the handle, or ram, pushed rapidly in, could propel that acorn at some velocity.

Whatever type of knife it was, there was never any thought of using it in anger, or against any person. Knives were a practical, useful, harmless part of a boy's belongings, something, at times, to help people you met rather than threaten them, and it is sad that modern society dictates that anyone found with a knife in their pocket today runs the risk of being arrested for carrying an offensive weapon. A pocket knife was as much a routine part of

A Childhood Like Ours…

the paraphernalia you had with you as your handkerchief, pocket money in pennies, threepenny bits and sixpences, pencils, string, or maybe a set of five-stones.

But back to walking. Often the walk up Bath Hills would continue through to Earsham, past the station and home over Earsham Dam. We reckoned it was about seven miles in all, and if we had gone in the morning we were usually late for dinner. I remember on one occasion getting caught in a torrential downpour as we came over the Dam, on the old road of course, just where the layby now is, and though we had coats on we were literally soaked to the skin, through coat, pullover, shirt and vest. Even the vest Mum was able to wring out.

You never minded getting wet, or dirty, of course, but for poor old Mum, with no luxury aids such as washing machines, and clothes washed in the kitchen sink with washing powder (Rinso, Oxydol or Persil, probably) or a bar of washing soap, it was a laborious task.

Another popular walk for us was up St Mary's Fields, which started when you crossed Hillside Road at that end of the Ups and Downs, the footpath linking it with Southend Road, and went right through to the road at St Margaret's where Manor Farm is situated. It was a beautiful walk, past fields which in summer were red with poppies, and beside which, in spring, ditches were full of primroses and violets. The Kings Road housing estate and the grammar school (now the high school) were not there then, and from the bedroom window at our home at Southend Road we had a panoramic view of the poppy fields. It was a good route along which to find blackberries in the autumn, and one which got pretty muddy in the winter.

It formed part of the course for the grammar school cross country running - the final part of a course which took runners from the school field in St John's Road, down Flixton Road, up

A Childhood Like Ours…

Constitution Hill, then over fields and ditches at the back of Upland Hall before getting back on to the road near Manor Farm - great fun, and the muddier you got the more you enjoyed it. I'd often run it on my own, after school.
The walk up St Mary's Fields was usually the outward part. More often than not, having regained the road at Manor Farm, we would walk either through to the Halesworth road and home down St John's Hill, or go in the other direction and home down St Margaret's Road and Flixton Road. It was usually a Sunday afternoon, and we got home just in time for tea, and raspberry jam sandwiches and Mum's delicious chocolate cake.
And then it was a case of doing school homework, which was usually left till Sunday evening…

A Childhood Like Ours…

Customs and Traditions

TODAY'S children will scarcely be back to school after the summer holidays when the first signs of Christmas appear in the bigger shops. Certainly three months before December 25th you can be forgiven for thinking Christmas is in full swing.

My recollection as a child of the 1950s is that there would be nothing in the shops to indicate Christmas before December 1st, and that was the date we counted down from to the great day. It seemed an age.

Mum would have catalogues - Gamage's and J D Williams are the ones I remember - full of toys and books of all kinds, and we would choose the ones we would like though with no promise of receiving them. Looking through those catalogues beside the open fire was one of the customs of our family and it brings back fond memories. No doubt parcels would arrive in due course, though we were at school when that happened so we had no idea whether things had been ordered or not. We simply looked forward excitedly.

Dad would bring the Christmas tree home only a few days before the day, and it would not be put in its pot and ready to decorate until Christmas Eve - there was no question of it being done two weeks beforehand, and it was a Christmas Eve task which kept we children occupied while Mum completed the final baking and other preparations.

That included the Christmas pudding and Christmas cake, which would have been made a few days beforehand, and it was a ritual that each of the children would have a stir of the mix, and make a wish as they did so, with eyes closed. If you revealed what you wished, the spell would be broken and the wish not granted. I have to admit those wishes were usually selfish - and usually to do with what present we wanted!

Back to Christmas Eve. During the day we may have gone up the town (into Bungay) and bought our presents for Dad and Mum and each other with our pocket money, if we had not got them already - inexpensive items inevitably, but meaningful we hoped - and would then wrap them when we got home, tying the parcels with string, Sellotape not being in general use at the time.

At around 4pm we would go off down to Bridge's (at the end of Southend Road, as mentioned elsewhere) and buy packs of coloured strips of paper for making decorations. As soon as tea was over, we could start making the trimmings from them, using paste made from water and flour, and linking each one in turn till we had enough lengths, and long enough, to criss-cross the dining room and the front room from corner to corner. They were supplemented with a few bell-shaped and ball shaped decorations.

That done, we could finally decorate the Christmas tree, getting the trimmings box from the cupboard where it had lain for the past 12 months, and putting them on as attractively and symmetrically as young children could. Strings of coloured electric lights as decorations had not been thought of then (certainly not in our house) - the decorations included candle-holders containing real candles, abut eight of them altogether, which were only lit on Christmas Day evening for about 20 minutes while we all sang carols round the tree to their flickering, cosy light - a wonderful, warm truly Christmas experience. That was repeated each evening for a few days.

So Christmas was set - there was no question of tree and decoration being put up before the evening of Christmas Eve,

A Childhood Like Ours…

and because of that it heightened the atmosphere of excitement and expectancy.

Helping prepare the Christmas cake was a particular joy - watching it being iced, watching mum put the little tree, and animals and crib on it, and scraping out the remains of the icing from the bowl with a spoon. It reminds me that there was another tradition in our house related to cooking - on the last day of each school holiday we would be allowed to do some cooking ourselves, under mum's guidance. We made simple items - small cakes, and pastry squares with currants and raisins in them. They were always edible - at least, we ate them ourselves!

In the calendar year the next tradition was Valentine's Day - not the sending of cards, but a visit from Valentine himself! I don't know how widespread it was but it was something looked forward to in our Bungay household. You would be sitting there, just after tea, on the day, when suddenly there would be a loud bang on the back door which made us jump out of our skins. But when you went to the door there was no one there - just a gift lying on the doorstep. You would grab it and close the door quickly.

Shortly after, the front door bell would ring loudly, you'd run and open it, with the same result - no one there, but a gift on the step.

This would happen three or four times at each door, and when things fell silent, each child would have an even share of gifts - nothing expensive, usually a packet of crisps, a packet of fruit gums, a note book and pencil, a small toy, and that sort of thing.

Of course each time Valentine called, Dad was late home from work, and came in soon after the excitement was all over!

It was a custom not widely observed, but one eagerly looked forward to in our family each year.

Next came Easter. Hot crossed buns on Good Friday seems such

A Childhood Like Ours...

a routine and ordinary thing today, partly because you see them in the shops weeks before the day - you can get them at almost anytime of the year. In the early 1950s they were something to look forward to on that one day of the year. They were ordered in advance and we looked forward excitedly to them, and were up early on Good Friday, to enjoy them, warm and toasted, for breakfast, after our bowl of Shredded Wheat, or Weetabix. In those days, hot crossed buns were an annual treat.

The Easter Egg hunt on Easter Day was a tradition which most families did follow in those days, I believe. It was always soon after breakfast, in the garden, and when given the word we rushed out to search frantically among the shrubs and plants and small trees, and on the rockery. We were looking for hard-boiled eggs on which Mum had painted patterns and faces with water colour paints. In those days there were no elaborate chocolate eggs encased in huge colourful cardboard boxes and produced by a range of chocolate companies. There were chocolate eggs though, which we were given when we got back indoors. They were clad in coloured silver paper and often contained a few chocolates. Sometimes we were given egg-shaped boxes with a gift in.

Gathering primroses was another tradition, around Easter time if Easter was late - today primroses appear in late February or even before but it was an April tradition in the 1950s. We would walk up St Mary's Fields, or up into the Saints via St Margaret's Road, and gather them from the deep ditches protected by well-maintained hawthorn hedges and blackberry bushes, to take home to Mum, who put them in jam-jar vases, perhaps with some sprigs of pussy willow or hazel catkins.

Those blackberry bushes would be the target in the autumn when the juicy black fruit was ripe. Usually we collected them in paper bags, and St Mary's Fields was our main walk to

A Childhood Like Ours…

collect them - in the 1950s the Common was not rampant with brambles as it is today.

With fingers purple with juice stains and full of bramble scratches - and probably blotched with a few nettle stings too - we took our bounty home to be weighed on the kitchen scales. Sometimes it would be as much as 3lb or 4lb, but there were often autumn reports of people collecting 12-15lbs of black berries in a good season.

If it was a weekend we would have stewed blackberries and custard for "afters" at dinner time on Sunday, with the dark purple juice and the yellow custard merging into a light, streaky mauve if you stirred them together. The bowl of sweet-tasting food took on the appearance of an evening summer sky when the sun is setting and light evening cloud turns it into what I still call today "a blackberries and custard sky" - a peaceful sky heralding a fine tomorrow…

A Childhood Like Ours…

And Then There Was…

The dump in Priory Lane, a huge dirty heap of rubbish - tyres, car parts, oily bits and pieces, papers, litter, cigarette packets, matchboxes. It was in the area to the right as you go into the lane from St Mary's Street, the site now covered by the British Legion club, the right-hand section of the car park, and the chalet bungalow beside it. I think it was probably the rubbish tip for the bus station and particularly the bus garage where maintenance was carried out on the vehicles, but no doubt others in the area deposited rubbish there, and my recollection of it is that as children we used to climb up it - it was maybe four or five feet high.

I remember it because I and my brother Robin went through a phase of collecting cigarette packets and matchbox tops, to see how many different ones we could get. We pasted them into scrap books. That tip was a great source of those items, often half buried in the grime - they may well have been among the litter left by passengers in the buses which was put on the tip when the vehicles were cleaned; some no doubt were discarded by the mechanics who worked there.

Whatever the source, we would eagerly scour the grime heap to find them - Craven A, Senior Service, Player's, Player's Weights, Wills Woodbines, Park Drive are some of the cigarette names I remember, and there were also some lesser known ones, which were particularly exciting to find. Swan Vestas and Ship were the common matchboxes, but it is surprising how many different ones we found - they filled several pages of a large scrap book which, regrettably, has long since gone to the scrap heap itself.

A Childhood Like Ours…

Collecting things was a regular hobby in the 1950s, and while it happens today it is mainly of items specifically made to collect, and somehow does not evoke the same fascination.

We were always playing in the rivers and streams around Bungay, and trying to dam the streams was often a holiday challenge. Our gang on Ditchingham Dam tried to do it on one of the dykes that flows under the Dam, and we almost achieved it, at its narrowest point as it flowed towards Douglas Farm.
Another favourite spot was in the woods, up beyond Constitution Hill off Flixton Road, where a stream flowed steeply down through the woods and, presumably, under the road when it reached it. That was a difficult task because the gradient meant the stream flowed quickly, but it was much narrower than the one under Ditchingham Dam, and sometimes we did manage to actually stem the flow, with a mixture of sticks and stones and earth and other debris gathered from the woods. The tall trees kept out much of the light from the sun and the undergrowth was always damp and ferny there in those woods, a beautiful spot for childhood play.

And then there were the various sandpits to play in - one up St Margaret's Road, one up St John's Hill, and one along Beccles Road, all sites where sand was extracted when needed for building work and other uses. In all three places it was soft and stone free, and we got huge enjoyment from clambering up from the bottom, and reaching the grassy "cliff top." From there there was a sheer drop of a few feet down to a lesser gradient of soft sand, and it was hugely exciting to run and jump from the top into that soft landing area and then roll a bit further down. Probably we were not supposed to be at any of those sites, but the thrill and the challenge of the jumping was too tempting, and

A Childhood Like Ours...

This picture, from 1950, is probably of the last fair to be held at Skinner's Meadow, or the Fairstead Meadow, in St John's Road.

we certainly did neither the sandpit nor ourselves and harm. Of course there was an element of risk - there is in any childhood activities - but we learned from it, and it was healthy outdoor activity that expended our energy and sent us home ravenous. The only "hurt" was a scolding when we arrived home with our clothes covered with sand and our shoes full of it!

We loved it when the fair or circus came to Outney Common. Stock's funfair would pitch there twice a year, with the whirr of its fairground rides, the scent of the candyfloss and fairground rock, the sparking of the dodge'em poles as they took their power from the roof of the track, the blaring music from the waltzers or carousel, the calling of the stallholders to "have a go" at whatever they were offering, the "chock" sound as a

A Childhood Like Ours…

wooden ball found its target at the coconut shy - all these created a heady atmosphere as we went there to spend our saved up pocket money. You could win goldfish on the hoopla stall, and many is the time we proudly went home with prize in a jam jar, then went up the town to get a small round tub of goldfish food to feed it. Sadly, and not unexpectedly, in those conditions, the fish never survived for many weeks. The dodge'ems were the favourite for young boys of course, and the name was a misnomer - despite the advice from the operator you always did your best to career into your friends, an achievement which gave all of you an abrupt juddering jolt. But you turned round and did it again.

Pennies and threepenny bits and sixpences changed hands at the stalls and rides as you went around the site, until you had spent out, and returned across the bridge, over the railway and on to the Little Common and home, with your bag of delicious rock in your pocket.

I can just remember one fair being held on the Fairstead Meadow - Skinner's Meadow - at St John Road, and I believe that was in 1950. And I'm sure it was before 1950 that I remember a circus and menagerie on the Common, with the abiding picture in my mind of an elephant eating a loaf of bread whole, and a lion in the ring under the big top.

*R*andom *memories, of days when life was routine and exciting in equal measure, when things which today may seem trivial and mundane captured our imagination and fuelled our thoughts and creativity, in Bungay, a rural market town in an era when there was time to dwell on things and enjoy them.*

Memories are limitless. Someone else could compile a book on

A Childhood Like Ours…

Bungay in the 1950s without mentioning any of the activities and thoughts and feelings included in these pages, and still fill an interesting volume.

But memories jog memories, and my hope is that those who read this will remember Bungay of the fifties in other ways, and be glad, too, that they grew up there…

The End